Taking the Red Pill
Seven Seasons of Buffy
Five Seasons of Angel
What Would Sipowicz Do?
Stepping through the Stargate
Finding Serenity
The War of the Worlds
Alias Assumed
Navigating the Golden Compass
Farscape Forever!
Flirting with Pride and Prejudice
Revisiting Narnia
Totally Charmed
King Kong Is Back!
Mapping the World of the Sorcerer's Apprentice
The Unauthorized X-Men
The Man from Krypton
Welcome to Wisteria Lane
Star Wars on Trial
The Battle for Azeroth
Boarding the Enterprise
Getting Lost
James Bond in the 21st Century
So Say We All
Investigating CSI
Webslinger
Halo Effect
Neptune Noir
Coffee at Luke's
Perfectly Plum
Grey's Anatomy 101
Serenity Found
House Unauthorized
Batman Unauthorized
Demigods and Monsters
In the Hunt
Flirtin' with the Monster
Mind-Rain

Leading
Science Fiction
Authors
on Douglas Adams'
The Hitchhiker's
Guide
to the Galaxy

The
Anthology
at the
End of the
Universe

EDITED BY
GLENN YEFFETH

An imprint of BenBella Books, Inc.
Dallas, TX

"Beware of the Leopard" © 2004 by Mike Byrne

"That About Wraps it Up for Oolon Colluphid" © 2004 by Don DeBrandt

"Wikipedia: A Genuine H2G2—Minus the Editors" © 2004 by Cory Doctorow

"The Secret Symbiosis" © 2004 by Bruce Bethke

"42" © 2004 by Adam Roberts

"A Consideration of Certain Aspects of Vogon Poetry" © 2004 by Lawrence Watt-Evans

"The Holy Trilogy" © 2004 by Selina Rosen

"The Zen of 42" © 2004 by Marie-Catherine Caillava

"Loop-Surface Security" © 2004 by Mark W. Tiedemann

"Yes, I Got It" © 2004 by Jacqueline Carey

"You Can't Go Home Again, Damn It!" © 2004 by Susan Sizemore

"The Subversive Dismal Scientist" © 2004 by Vox Day

"Lunching at the Eschaton" © 2004 by Stephen Baxter

"Digital Watches May Be a Pretty Neat Idea, but Peanuts and Beer Are What Get You Through the Apocolypse" © 2004 by A. M. Dellamonica

"The Only Sane Man in the Universe" © 2004 by Marguerite Krause

"Douglas Adams and the Wisdom of Madness" © 2004 by John Shirley

"A Talk with Douglas Adams" © 2004 by John Shirley

"Another Fine Mess" © 2004 by Adam-Troy Castro

"Words to Live By" © 2004 by Amy Berner

"'Goodnight, Marvin'" © 2004 by Maria Alexander

Additional materials © 2004 BenBella Books

Smart Pop is an imprint of BenBella Books, Inc.
10440 N. Central Expressway, Suite 800
Dallas, TX 75206
www.benbellabooks.com
Send feedback to feedback@benbellabooks.com
BenBella and Smart Pop are federally registered trademarks.

Printed in the United States of America

Library of Congress Cataloging-in-Publication data is available for this title.
ISBN 978-1932100-56-3

Cover design by Melody Cadungog
Text design and composition by John Reinhardt Book Design

Contents

Beware of the Leopard   1
Mike Byrne

That About Wraps it Up for Oolon Colluphid   11
Don DeBrandt

Wikipedia: A Genuine H2G2—Minus the Editors   25
Cory Doctorow

The Secret Symbiosis: The Hitchhiker's Guide to the
Galaxy and Its Impact on Real Computer Science   35
Bruce Bethke

42   47
Adam Roberts

A Consideration of Certain Aspects of Vogon Poetry   65
Lawrence Watt-Evans

The Holy Trilogy   73
Selina Rosen

The Zen of 42   83
Marie-Catherine Caillava

Loop-Surface Security: The Image of the Towel in a
Vagabond Universe—A Semiotic (Semi-Odd) Excursion   97
Mark W. Tiedemann

Yes, I Got It   105
Jacqueline Carey

You Can't Go Home Again, Damn It! Even If Your
Planet Hasn't Been Blown Up by Vogons   111
Susan Sizemore

The Subversive Dismal Scientist: Douglas Adams
and the Rule of Unreason   117
  Vox Day

Lunching at the Eschaton: Douglas Adams and the
End of the Universe in Science Fiction.   125
  Stephen Baxter

Digital Watches May Be a Pretty Neat Idea, But Peanuts
and Beer Are What Get You Through the Apocalypse   133
  A. M. Dellamonica

The Only Sane Man in the Universe   145
  Marguerite Krause

Douglas Adams and the Wisdom of Madness   157
  John Shirley

A Talk with Douglas Adams   169
  John Shirley

Another Fine Mess   179
  Adam-Troy Castro

Words to Live By   187
  Amy Berner

"Goodnight, Marvin"   197
  Maria Alexander

Mike Byrne

The Hitchhiker's Guide to the Galaxy was released before Windows, before $200 stereo systems came with remote controls, before elevators spoke to us, before, in essence, computers took over our lives. Most of us jumped into the computer revolution with enthusiasm, only to find ourselves spending increasing amounts of time each day dealing with technology and its foibles. We can't say we weren't warned.

FOR YEARS RADIOS HAD BEEN OPERATED by means of pressing buttons and turning dials; then as the technology became more sophisticated the controls were made touch-sensitive—you merely had to brush the panels with your fingers; now all you had to do was wave your hand in the general direction of the components and hope. It saved a lot of muscular expenditure, of course, but meant that you had to sit infuriatingly still if you wanted to keep listening to the same program.

ANYONE WHO DOUBTS that we are on the road that Douglas Adams laid out in the above passage would do well to take a look at aftermarket car stereos which now frequently include remote controls. Once a remote control is necessary to operate a device which is itself within arm's reach, the battle over whether we or our devices are in control has clearly turned sharply in favor of the devices. I once asked a car stereo salesman why one anyone would want a remote for something they could already reach, and this answer really got to the root of the problem: the remote was useful because the stereo itself had too many buttons which were too small to actually operate while driving.

"So you get the remote," I conjectured, "because the design of the thing it controls is so bad that a separate, simpler set of controls is necessary?"

"Er, yes," came the hesitant reply.

"So why not," I patiently asked, "put the large and usable controls on the stereo in the first place?"

"Because then you'd lose all these great features!"

"How often," I wondered aloud, "do you really need to mess with all those other features?"

He pondered this for a moment. "Well, only once really, when you first set it up."

"Let me see if I have this straight: the remote control is a good thing because the stereo itself is unusable, which in turn is necessary in order to support a set of functions I'll never use again—have I got that right?"

"Look, mister, *I* didn't design it!" Suddenly, there was urgent business elsewhere in the television section of the store.

One of the jobs of the science fiction writer is, in a sense, to forecast the future, particularly the future of technology and its effects on society. Thus, science fiction is replete with extreme visions, both utopian and apocalyptic (for a fine set of considerations of the dark and dysto-pian end of the scale, see *Taking the Red Pill* and similar commentary on movies like *The Matrix*). Douglas Adams, however, always struck me as a humorist as much as a science fiction author. The problem with try-ing to be both a humorist and a sci-fi writer is that neither utopias nor apocalypses are particularly funny. Adams had a great talent for seeing a different kind of high-tech world, one not characterized by either de-humanization and fear or ideal perfection, but rather characterized by annoyance. Maybe this is an alternate form of dystopia; not dark slavery or warfare with the machines, but a huge increase in the small daily annoyances we have engineered for ourselves. What often makes such systems funny is their obvious plausibility. It is not hard to imagine many of our current annoyances playing out in the future just as Adams describes. We identify with the trials of Arthur Dent because so many of them don't feel all that distant from the trials we experience every day.

I know I personally identify greatly with such frustrations. Small (and sometimes not so small) annoyances and my inability to gracefully tol-erate them are, in part, what led me to my choice of academic discipline. My Ph.D. is in psychology, but don't be misled by that. Despite media presentations to the contrary, a large percentage of people out there with advanced training in psychology are *not* of the "lie on the couch and tell me about your mother" variety. My area is cognitive psychology, which is the scientific study of perception, attention, memory, language, deci-sion making, problem solving and the like. I also have degrees in engi-neering and computer science. What unifies all this is work in a domain known by names like *human factors* and *ergonomics*. Most people in the U.S. associate ergonomics with things like the design of chairs and key-boards to avoid repetitive stress injuries, which are indeed part of that endeavor, but overall it is much wider than that. Human factors profes-sionals study the interaction of humans with all kinds of systems, from simple consumer products all the way up to air transportation systems and nuclear power plants. A popular and rapidly growing domain is, of course, computer systems.

I think one of the formative experiences for me was hearing about a text editor (which is like a word processor with slightly different goals) in the pre-mouse-and-Windows days. This editor, like many editors of its time, was modal, meaning that the same keys had different mean-ings depending on what mode the system was in. In this particular system, the editor was invoked by typing "edit" in the command line. The program was an advanced one which supported a number of advanced features not commonly found in editors of its day; it even had an "undo" command which would undo the last edit. The program had, however, one particularly noxious design flaw in it: in one of the command modes, typing the word "edit" caused the user to irrevocably lose the entire document on which he or she was working! This sounds like something that Arthur Dent would have done on a regular basis.

How could this possibly come about, not in a work of fiction, but in the real world? Well, "e" was the command to select the <u>e</u>ntire document, "d" was the command to <u>d</u>elete the current selection, "i" was the command to change into text <u>i</u>nsertion mode, and the "t" was simply inserted as text. "Undo" could be invoked at this point, which would undo the last edit: the "t" would be removed. Taken locally, each one of the choices for commands seems reasonable, but the final combination of commands was profoundly unfriendly to real users. It was experiences with systems like this that caused me to consider studying how people work to better support the better design of man-made systems. Until something is done, we will continue to have a world filled with the kind of things which inhabit Arthur's world:

> [Arthur] reached out and pressed an invitingly large red button on a nearby panel. The panel lit up with the words *Please do not press this button again*. He shook himself.

There is probably some context in which the design choices made by system designers, including Arthur's unfriendly button, seem reasonable. Most designers are not misanthropes, so why is our world filled with technological systems which are so badly matched to us? The problem is that there is no one single reason, but rather a myriad of factors which contribute to unusable, unsafe or otherwise un-optimal systems—the kind of systems which Arthur seemed inexorably to run afoul of. One contributing factor is that many technologists are simply fascinated by solving technical problems, regardless of whether or not anyone else wants or needs the solutions to those problems. I managed to annoy numerous computer science colleagues in graduate school by asking them to explain to me why they were doing the research they were doing.

"Oh, it's this great interesting problem…" was often the beginning of the reply.

"Yes," I'd agree, even if it wasn't, "but who's going to make use of it? What's it actually good for?" The frequency with which such questions brought about stunned silence would give anyone who's pressuring his

or her child to major in computer science significant pause. "Because
we can" is not an adequate answer to the question "Why is that feature
being added?" For example:

> "Listen," said Ford, who was still engrossed in the sales bro-
> chure, "they make a big thing of the ship's cybernetics. *'A new gen-
> eration of Sirius Cybernetics Corporation robots and computers, with
> the new GPP feature.'"*
> "GPP feature?" said Arthur. "What's that?"
> "Oh, it says *Genuine People Personalities."*
> "Oh," said Arthur, "sounds ghastly."
> A voice behind them said, "It is."

In some twisted way the idea of GPPs always reminds me of the "DSP
modes" found in home theater equipment. This is the series of buttons
on the stereo with labels like "cathedral" and "amphitheater" which cause
the audio signal to be processed by a computer to simulate what it would
sound like in the named environment. Is there anybody out there who
really needs to know how, say, *The Fifth Element* would have sounded if
he or she had seen it inside a cathedral? Just because clever electrical engineers can build such devices doesn't mean we really need them.

But the fault does not always rest with the system designers, either.
Often part of the problem rests with those who oversee the designers. I
had a colleague—more accurately, a drinking buddy at conferences—in
graduate school who, upon completion of his degree, went to work for a
major software firm whose products were (and still are) used incredibly
widely and were, at the time, routinely lambasted for poor usability.

"How could you," I asked him while waiting in line at the bar, "go to
work for them? How can they be so blind to how bad things are?"

"No," he shook his head, "they aren't blind. Everybody on the
design team knows how awful [the program suite] is. But it doesn't
matter, because marketing calls all the shots. We have to add X new
features on a short deadline because they say those things have to be
there to justify charging massive upgrade fees, which leaves no time
to design them well or fix other problems." What I failed to realize at
the time is that this was for many years an incredibly successful business strategy; rather than being disgusted, I should have borrowed
money to buy this company's stock. The fact is that many systems are
bad because we allow them to be. We tolerate things we shouldn't because many of us don't realize it doesn't actually have to be that bad.

This seems particularly true in the computer domain, and of course in Arthur's world:

> [Arthur] had found a Nutri-Matic machine which had provided him with a plastic cup filled with a liquid that was almost, but not quite, entirely unlike tea. The way it functioned was very interesting. When the *Drink* button was pressed, it made an instant but highly detailed examination of the subject's taste buds.... However, no one was sure why it did this because it invariably delivered a cupful of liquid that was almost, but not quite, entirely unlike tea.

Another factor driving mal-designed systems is that the technologists designing the systems simply do not have a clear understanding of how humans work. They lack detailed knowledge about the amount of force the human back can endure in an eight-hour shift or how the human cognitive system takes shortcuts to reduce cognitive load. When a problem arises, the proffered solution is a redesign of the human element, not the mismatched system. One of my favorite examples of this is the history of design of automated teller machines (ATMs).

People have a strong tendency to discontinue activity related to a goal once that goal has been met. This leads to a number of systematic errors which involve performing some steps after the goal of a task is satisfied. One of the "classic" examples of this is leaving one's bankcard in the ATM. The main goal of the task (get cash) has been satisfied, but there's another step (remove the card) to be performed after that goal has been satisfied. This manifests in other kinds of slips, such as forgetting the original document on the photocopier or leaving off the gas cap after filling up the car. These errors are so pervasive that they often have to be "designed out" of the system. For example, on most cars the gas cap is now attached to the car so that it cannot be completely forgotten.

In the first generation of ATMs (at least in most of the United States), banks quickly discovered that a large number of patrons left their cards in ATMs, which not only annoyed consumers but cost the banks a lot of money in administrative overhead, deactivating lost cards, fixing balances for fraudulent withdrawals, issuing new cards and the like. (My father works in information technology for a major bank and I'm quite confident that if customer annoyance had been the only consequence, nothing would have changed.) The solution, the designers decided, was not to change the system so that the task was structured in a way which better matched how people think, but rather to try to "correct" the "faulty" human element: the systems emitted a loud and annoying series of beeps after the cash was dispensed. This did somewhat reduce the incidence of left-behind bankcards but not nearly enough to cover the cost to the banks of the lost cards. Most current ATMs now prevent this error entirely by requiring that the card be withdrawn before cash is dispensed or never taking possession of the card in the first place (e.g., using a swipe).

System designers, who often have to be experts in a technical domain such as computer programming or electrical engineering, simply fail to fully appreciate the human element. It's not always their fault; it's just outside their area of expertise. There seems to be a permeating belief that if the correct state can be reached by the user at all, no matter how twisted the route, that's good enough. A colleague of mine met one of the engineers responsible for the flight management computer systems found in many large commercial aircraft. These systems, while very capable (they save airlines millions of dollars a year in fuel costs), are notoriously difficult for pilots to program correctly—fortunately for us passengers, pilots are generally dedicated and highly skilled and can usually ably recover from such errors. But the fact that such errors are so common puzzled the engineer. He told my colleague something along the lines of, "I don't understand what the problem is. All the pilots have to do is memorize all 227 modes...." Usable for the system designer simply doesn't cut it from the point of view of the user, who of course in Adams' world was usually poor Arthur:

> "But the plans were on display..."
> "On display? I eventually had to go down to the cellar to find them."
> "That's the display department."
> "With a flashlight."
> "Ah, well, the lights had probably gone."
> "So had the stairs."
> "But look, you found the notice, didn't you?"
> "Yes," said Arthur, "yes I did. It was on display in the bottom of a locked filing cabinet stuck in a disused lavatory with a sign on the door saying 'Beware of the Leopard.'"

Another reason for the persistence of hard-to-use designs is that often usability takes a backseat to some other consideration which trades off against it. Sometimes, to make something truly useful, aesthetics have to be compromised. Often, designers are unwilling to make this compromise. This kind of design trade-off is easy to see on the World Wide Web (one can only imagine the field day Adams would have had with the Web). Many Web sites, upon first arrival of the user, display a beautiful though truly useless bit of animation, forcing the user to wait to get where he or she is trying to go. Frustration with these start-up animations has resulted in wide propagation of "skip intro" links included on such sites. This at least allows the user a little more control, but allowing more control is clearly not the primary design goal when forcing the user to sit through an animation which he or she did not request.

My younger brother is trained as a graphic designer, and discussions with him about what he was taught make it clear that there is small army of people out there who are explicitly instructed that considerations like keeping within the corporate color scheme are more important than usability concerns like making the location of clickable buttons obvious. When observing users surfing the Web, it is common to see people push the cursor all around the page just to see where it will turn into a little hand so they can determine which things can be clicked on at all. The fact that people naturally develop this strategy through even fairly brief exposures to the Web indicates that something is clearly amiss—usability has clearly taken a backseat. For a really terrific illustration of these, I highly recommend a trip to www.webpagesthatsuck.com. There is an entire section on the site—cleverly termed "mystery meat navigation"—devoted to the problem of unclear controls. Adams provides one of my all-time favorite examples of design in which aesthetics trumps usability. It's funny because it's only slightly more extreme than things we interact with every day:

> "It's the wild color scheme that freaks me," said Zaphod whose love affair with this ship had lasted almost three minutes into the flight. "Every time you try to operate one of these weird black controls that are labeled in black on a black background, a little black light lights up black to let you know you've done it."

I don't mean to paint too negative a picture of system designers; many systems are designed well and perform their functions safely, easily and efficiently, and their designers should be commended on their fine work. However, it does seem that there is no shortage of examples where that is not the case. In my undergraduate human factors course, a few of the homework assignments I give are what I call "show-and-tell" assignments. Students are to find an example of a poorly designed system or device and present it to the class. Once students become attuned to looking for such things, the gusto with which these assignments are attacked is impressive. Also amazing is the range of things which students come up with: unreadable wristwatches, badly designed car seats, error-prone alarm clocks, unserviceable vending machines, horrific remote controls, confusing signage at intersections, espresso machines which appear to have "burn the users' fingers" as a major design goal, mobile phones with impenetrable menu structures, doors which require being simultaneously pushed and pulled to open—the list goes on and on. These designs are often so bad that early in the course, fellow students require a great deal of convincing that the system really exists in that horrible form; I had to start requiring that students provide photographs because too many examples were simply too awful to be believable. Adams would have been unable to use most of these things in his books because readers simply would not think it possible that such things existed or could exist in an even more high-tech universe. But examples of badly designed objects and systems are easy to come by, and there's no compelling reason to believe that such things are going to go away as technology advances. Residents of Adams' galaxy have mastered interstellar space travel but still have to contend with depressed elevators and centuries-long waits for lemon-soaked paper napkins.

Systems designed to make our lives easier in one respect, even when effective in that regard, often seem inexorably to introduce problems in other areas. Electronic mail has undoubtedly enabled all kinds of communication and conveniences that were hard to imagine prior to its introduction—I can hardly imagine living without it at this point. But even e-mail has its drawbacks, as anyone who has to wade through thousands of "spam" messages or gotten a virus from such things can attest. Those kinds of problems stem from malevolent use of the system, but sometimes problems arise simply because it is very difficult to engineer large, complex, distributed systems in such a way that they are completely reliable. And managing that unreliability seems a breeding ground for Adams-style mishaps. Here's an excerpt from a message sent out by mail system administrators after a mail outage at a university (which I came across at http://www.netfunny.com/rhf/jokes/04/Nov/truenews.html):

> We are currently experiencing intermittent problems receiving external mail. We have corrected the problem, but the changes will not take effect until replication to external sources completes. If you have not received messages, please have the sender resend the message to ensure delivery.

How exactly mail system users were to figure out which e-mails were lost so that they could contact the senders was not apparent—perhaps a Sub-Etha Sens-O-Matic or an Infinite Improbability Drive could be useful in such circumstances. It certainly seems infinitely improbable to me that my university will ever have a class registration system which is not error-prone and inefficient. In my six years here we are now on our third such system, each one no better, and in many circumstances worse, than the previous system. I have to chuckle at the idea of Arthur Dent registering for a class here and have no doubt that an attempt to register for, say, "Feminist Social Thought" would end up with Mr. Dent actually registered for "Biochemical Engineering," since they both come up when one searches for course number 460.

Obviously, there are many other sources of humor in the Hitchhiker's Guide series besides all the follies with technology. But such follies are likely to stand the test of time and remain humorous for many years to come, because the things that lead to technologies being mismatched to humans show no signs of remission. A couple years ago my department got a new photocopier which came with a manual roughly eighteen inches thick, because, the sales guy assured us, of all the fabulous things it could do. Never minding the fact that none of us were likely to ever want to use most of those features, the salesman—I think his name was Phil—plunged on with his demonstration. Someone asked how to perform some kind of interleaving that our old copier could do and, of course, the new copier could do it as well—sort of. After Phil had pressed some dozen or so buttons to try to get the machine into the mode that would do the requested task, one of my fellow professors, a neuroscientist, turned to me and said, "You human factors people will *never* be out of a job." Similarly, many of the troubles encountered by people in the Guide series will probably always be funny, because they'll always hit a little too close to home.

Mike Byrne is an assistant professor of psychology at Rice University in Houston, Texas, though he grew up in Minneapolis, Minnesota. An avid reader of science fiction and fantasy since grade school, he has an advanced love-hate relationship with all forms of technology, particularly computers. Mike's research is focused on computer simulation of human cognition and performance in order to better understand how to design technology which more effectively meshes with human capabilities. His two boys, ages four years and six months, occupy the bulk of his limited free time.

Don DeBrandt

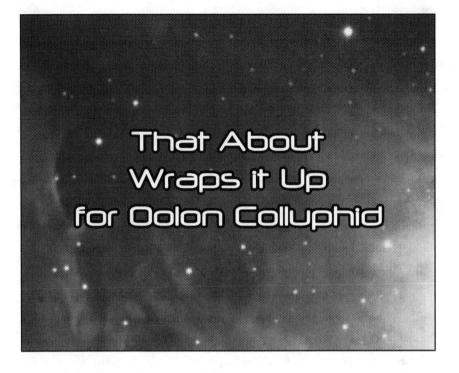

That About Wraps it Up for Oolon Colluphid

When Don proposed writing this essay, he described it as follows: "I intend to prove that God not only exists in Adams' universe, but identify who he is, explain what his plans are and reveal once and for all why he seems to be obsessed with fish. The explanation I've cleverly worked out involves time-travel, the Sirius Cybernetics Corporation, Eddies in the space-time continuum and how he got there. The number forty-two turns out to be surprisingly relevant in a very real way . . . ."

There's nothing I can possibly add to that, so here you go.

THE FIVE-PART HITCHHIKER'S GUIDE TRILOGY deals with many things: cosmology, the causes of war, alien cultures, artificial life, the unreliability of number-based logic systems—so many things, in fact, that an essayist considering how to tackle this towering edifice of concepts feels rather like a climber surveying Everest armed with a roadside map, a length of clothesline and a committee of blind Sherpas; you possess at least rudimentary equipment, the bloody thing isn't hard to find, and the overall consensus seems to be in favor of the direction "up"... but somehow, in deciding exactly which route to take, the whole process gets a bit bogged down.

So, some words about fish.

Now, you may think that an essay dealing with such lofty ideas as the Existence of God (and rest assured, this is exactly such an essay; if you're looking for mindless entertainment and a few cheap laughs go download some presidential quotes, 'cause this is Serious Philosophical Stuff) has no place discussing anything with gills.

You would, however, be staggeringly wrong.

Fish occupy an extremely important place in the Adams universe. A somewhat damp place, it must be admitted, but important nonetheless. What is it that the lead singer of Disaster Area—the loudest rock band in existence—requires a doctor, a logician and a marine biologist to prove that he is not? A fish. What is it that the Ruler of the Universe offers to his hypothetical cat? A bit of fish. What is it that Arthur Dent views nervously when offered by Ford Prefect? Well, his hand, but he's nervous because it might turn out to *be* a fish. This reaction may have something to do with the fact that he's been living alone on prehistoric Earth for five years and talking to trees, but is more likely related to the "horrid fish" that rain from the sky when he and Ford are first picked up by the Improbability Drive, followed closely by Arthur's limbs falling off and Ford turning into a penguin.

Fish, of course, are a well-known symbol of Christianity. In the Hitchhiker books, they frequently represent the preternatural—as in the fish with a head at both ends, caught by Kirp in *Mostly Harmless*, with a head at both ends. This miracle, unfortunately, is cast into a somewhat doubtful light when Kirp's second two-headed fish turns out to be an obvious fake, but this merely makes it a religious symbol as opposed to a divine one.

Questions of subaquatic theology abound: Does the existence of the

Babel fish, a mind-bogglingly useful little creature that functions as a universal translator, prove the non-existence of God? If God does exist, is there a fish Heaven? And where did all the dolphins bugger off to, anyway?

The answers are A) no, B) yes and C) they aren't actually fish, so they fall beyond the scope of this essay.

Let us consider these questions in more depth. The famous Babel fish argument goes as follows: God refuses to prove he exists, because proof denies faith and without faith he is nothing. However, since the Babel fish is much too specifically useful to have evolved by chance, it proves the existence of God—which by his own admission reduces him to zero.

This argument, while brilliantly logical, only works if God plays by the rules. As there are many examples of God not only cheating but being a right bastard and blaming it on someone else, it simply doesn't hold up—at least, it doesn't hold up the part it was meant to. What it does establish is that God not only exists, he's probably a Pisces.

As for a marine afterlife, many religious texts (including *So Long, and Thanks for All the Fish*) make reference to The Land Where Fish Are Eternally Blessed. These texts can be found in upscale scuba shops and aquarium boutiques across the galaxy, and are usually—but not always—waterproof.

Which brings us to robots.

Now, the connection between the two might not be immediately clear. This is a good thing—at least from my point of view—because if it were, this essay would be pointless and I wouldn't get paid. Happily, the line of reasoning that starts at "goes well with tartar sauce" and ends at "your plastic pal who's fun to be with" is convoluted and not at all obvious, which means that eventually I'll be able to go to a restaurant where they serve you sushi on a little conveyor belt.

The line about the plastic pal, as many of you will recognize, is one of the slogans of the Sirius Cybernetics Corporation. Another of their slogans is "Share and Enjoy!", usually chirped by a Nutri-Matic vending machine immediately after dispensing a cup of liquid that is "almost, but not quite, entirely unlike tea."

The reason it does this, I believe, is simple: the Sirius Cybernetics Corporation has as its ultimate goal the destruction of all life in the universe.

It has thus far failed for two reasons. One, because it is spectacularly incompetent; and two, because it is opposed in its efforts by another entity, which I will reveal just before you've gotten fed up with all the suspense and skipped ahead.

The Guide has this to say about SCC products: "—their fundamental design flaws are completely hidden by their superficial design flaws." Such as, for instance, the inability to make tea—not a flaw, but actually a feature. The reason it's doing this is to actually stop life from arising at all, a condition directly attributable to the Infinite Improbability Drive, which created said life simply by rearranging a few molecules in the distant past. The Drive itself was created by hooking a Bambleweeny 57 Sub-Meson Brain to an atomic vector plotter suspended in a strong Brownian motion producer—in this case, a cup of hot tea. The SCC, using flawless logic, reasoned that eliminating any of the elements in this equation would destroy the chain of events that led to the rise of life, and chose tea as the easiest link to sever. The fact that *any* cup of hot liquid will produce strong Brownian motion does not seem to have been considered, but probably would have once all tea had been eliminated and life stubbornly continued to exist.

When Arthur Dent tries to convince a Nutri-Matic to make some *actual* tea, he unknowingly sets in motion the greatest conflict to ever congeal in the thick gravy of the space-time continuum.

The *Heart of Gold*'s computer devotes all of its computational power to solving this problem, trying to find a way to counter the Nutri-Matic's hidden programming to *eliminate* all tea. Meanwhile, the Nutri-Matic—which functions by directly accessing the neural pathways of the subject's brain—has deduced that Arthur Dent's brain holds the Question to the Answer of the Life, the Universe and Everything. This is its true purpose, anyway; you don't make a drinks dispenser telepathic unless you have an ulterior motive. It's been said that if the Answer and the Question are ever both known at the same time, the universe will disappear (to be replaced immediately by something even more bizarre and inexplicable), and the Answer is already known: forty-two.

(It should be noted that on page forty-two of *The Hitchhiker's Guide to the Galaxy* it's mentioned that one of the things that desperately worry Ford Prefect are the terrible number of things human beings *don't* know about. Since Arthur is in fact unaware that his brain holds the Ultimate Question, this verges on foreshadowing—two or threeshadowing, perhaps.)

In any case, pulling the Question from Arthur's brain is another way of ending the universe, which will pretty well do it for life as well. That this does not in fact occur would imply that the ship's computer is successful, but it does not illustrate the true depth and breadth of this struggle. This is not a mere programming conflict—this is a battle between two immense intellects, both of which have access to technology so advanced as to be considered godlike. Now, this may seem like overstating the case a bit for a glorified soda machine, but the Nutri-Matic is only a single mechanical limb of a far more insidious cybernetic creature, which is no doubt in contact with it through the medium of the Sub-Etha network. But who is this being? Why does he want to destroy, well, Life, the Universe and Everything?

Because, of course, it was what he was programmed to do. Yes, the being in question is Hactar, the supercomputer built by the Silastic Armorfiends of Striterax and ordered to design the Ultimate Weapon. It created a hyperspace network meant to connect all stars together simultaneously, thus causing a universe-wide supernova (and if you can plug every sun in existence into the same outlet, you certainly have the ability to share information with a few vending machines) but, somewhat astoundingly, introduced a flaw into the device that would cause it not to function. It later tried to correct this flaw, even though it was now in a semi-gaseous state, and fulfill its original purpose.

The fact that it tried to bring about the End of All That Is (and if *that* phrase doesn't deserve capitals, I don't know what does) isn't hard to believe; it was simply doing what it was created to do. The real question is: what stopped it in the first place?

This is where it gets a bit tricky.

The problem with discussing time travel is that the whole notion of cause and effect becomes somewhat muddled; what starts out as a specific and demonstrable chain of events rapidly intertwines with super-string parallel universes, knots of paradox and recursive loops of braided space-time, quickly coming to resemble that snarled lump of old Mardi Gras necklaces, discarded shoelaces and useful six-inch lengths of wire in the bottom of your kitchen drawer. So, in the interests of clarity, I will try to limit my explanation to "who," as opposed to the harder-to-define "when," the ever-difficult "why" and the nearly impossible "how."

It was Marvin.

This is, as Marvin himself would say, depressingly obvious to anyone with an IQ above that of a Bugblatter Beast, a creature slightly more intelligent than a Republican voter. Of the four demonstrated times Marvin has interfaced with another computer system, one went into a serious funk, two committed outright suicide—well, the Frogstar tank killed itself more out of outraged stupidity than depression, but to be fair they only shared a brief verbal exchange rather than any serious bandwidth—and the fourth illustrates a decidedly different point. Still, these examples are persuasive enough to suggest that if anyone could convince a computer that destroying the universe simply wasn't worth the bother, it would be Marvin.

The fourth example takes place in *The Restaurant At The End Of The Universe*. Marvin talks to a Sirius Cybernetics Corporation Happy Vertical People Transporter (an elevator) and convinces it to go up despite it wanting very much not to. It does this, it claims, because it *likes* him—very odd indeed. And when Zaphod says, "You know something?" Marvin replies, "More than you can possibly imagine."

This transpires, it should be noted, on page forty-two.

SCC elevators possess limited precognition. The only reason an elevator that can predict the future would interface with Marvin—and like it—would be if it could see a quick, merciful death in its immediate future...which, after the Frogstar fighters attack the HHG building, is probably exactly what occurs.

Not all machines are so sanguine about their own doom, though. Hactar's decision to not blow up the universe gets it destroyed by its own builders—however, it doesn't let a little thing like being pulverized into dust stop it. Demonstrating not only a truly Halliburtonian talent for shaping entire civilizations but a willingness to alter history itself to accomplish its ends, it plants a supernova bomb in Arthur's bag, along with a compulsion for him to travel back in time to the Earth and set it off via hurling it at one of the Krikkit robots. This might seem like something of a convoluted plan...but only to a primitive humanoid descended from fish by way of monkeys. To a millennia-old supercomputer with a brain the size of a nebula, it's about as complicated as making a BLT—no bacon, hold the lettuce.

Fortunately, this plan is defeated by what at first glance would seem to be a happy accident; Arthur trips over his own bag. Under more careful scrutiny, though, an entire chain of events, stretching through both space and time, become clear.

(This is where it gets a bit tangled. If you get confused, go have a nice cup of Earl Grey, do a little light housework, and come back when you run into something you'd rather put off.)

Arthur trips over the bag, which sends him hurtling into the air. He winds up flying, which lets him defeat the robot and *not* destroy the universe. He learned how to do this the last time he saw an entirely different bag, which is when he was being chased by a landslide just after being teleported through time and space to the cave of Agrajag, the reincarnated being who hates Arthur Dent with a passion. This bag disappeared years ago when Arthur traveled to Greece, and its reappearance causes him to fall to the ground and miss.

Go. Put the kettle on. I'll wait.

Back for more, are you? Very well—but if you're allergic to the words "wouldn't" or "hadn't," I'd pop a few antihistamines right now.

If Arthur hadn't seen his missing bag, he wouldn't have learned to fly. If he hadn't learned to fly, he wouldn't have defeated the robot, thus not destroying the universe. He wouldn't have seen the bag if Agrajag hadn't diverted his teleportation, which wouldn't have happened if Agrajag hadn't been killed by Arthur over and over, causing his intense hatred. And the entire sequence wouldn't have occurred if Arthur's bag hadn't mysteriously made its way from a baggage terminal in Greece to a rocky hillside on the other side of the galaxy, an event with no clear explanation—except for the phrase uttered by Ford Prefect shortly before he and Arthur chase a floating sofa across a field: "Eddies in the space-time continuum."

Arthur's response of, "Ah. Is he? Is he?" is in fact completely correct. Eddy, the *Heart of Gold*'s computer, is not only *in* the space-time continuum, he is in large part in control of it.

Douglas Adams stated on more than one occasion that he was an atheist. He also stated that the idea of religion and deities fascinated him, which is why we find so many references to them in his books—Thor, Zarquon, Almighty Bob, the Great Green Arkleseizure. And if you're looking for God in the Hitchhiker's series, you don't have to look much further than Eddy (well, *slightly* further, but bear with me).

Eddy can use the Improbability Drive to do almost anything. Its reach extends through space *and* time—he uses it to send Arthur, Ford, Zaphod and Trillian to Milliways, the Restaurant at the End of the Universe, and to transport Zaphod and Marvin to the offices of the Hitchhiker's Guide. His power to affect probabilities means Eddy is close to omnipotent; the ghost of Zaphod's great great-grandfather tells Zaphod flat out, "The Improbability Field controls you, you are in its grip."

It's the Improbability Field that lets Eddy shrink the ship so Zaphod can carry it around in his pocket, and it's the Improbability Field that moves Arthur's bag from a luggage carousel in Athens to the middle of an avalanche on another planet, many years later—which leads, inevitably, to the salvation of the universe.

All this, mind you, over Arthur's desire for a cup of tea. No wonder Prak, the journalist who knows all the Truths of existence, is almost paralyzed by laughter when he meets him.

Since tea itself is not possible without life, Eddy has found himself embroiled in a war that rages across the depth and breadth of reality—a long, dark teatime of the soul. And despite the cybernetic nature of the battle, souls are definitely involved—most specifically, the soul of Marvin.

Marvin's most frequent complaint is that he's never given anything to challenge his intellect. Everyone around him is, in his estimation, almost infinitely stupid in comparison.

And he is absolutely correct.

"Brain the size of a planet" is often how he refers to himself. Since Marvin himself is *not* the size of a planet, this can only mean that—much like the pan-dimensional beings that manifest as white mice—Marvin's body is only a peripheral, an extrusion into the realm of the physical. His actual mind is located in hyperspace—and of *course* it's huge. This is the computer that controls the Infinite Improbability Drive, that has to calculate the largest numbers in existence. It's the mind that runs the important systems of the *Heart of Gold*—though, sadly, not the secondary ones.

Nobody ever notices this.

They simply encounter Marvin on the ship, assume he's an ordinary robot, and treat him as such—which is a lot like running into Einstein in a chip shop and asking him to make you a prawn curry. An extremely negative Einstein, mind you, one that would probably quote the latest statistics on Mad Cow disease and then suggest a nice roast beef sandwich instead, but still.

"What are you supposed to do when you *are* a manically-depressed robot?" Marvin says at one point.

You might assume someone would then think to ask, "When, exactly, does the *manic* part come in?" If they did, Marvin would tell them that Eddy, the perennially upbeat ship's computer, functions as the embodiment of that part of him...but no one ever does.

So when we're talking about Marvin, we're really talking about a pan-dimensional intelligence with a conflicted dual personality. There's a reason for this duality, but I'm of two minds as to whether I should reveal it just yet or not....

Sorry.

Marvin is almost always present at critical junctures of the plot. He gets Zaphod to his critical meeting with Zarniwoop, he stops the Krikkit robots from killing Zaphod (three times), and he saves the whole group from the trigger-happy Blagulon Kappa cops *and* from perishing in Disaster Area's Sundive ship. How Marvin survived this last adventure is never adequately explained, either…but it does lead to his leg being replaced by a cosmic artifact of immense power.

The explanation is quite simple: he was saved by the Improbability Field, which can warp reality—in fact, it transforms a desert into a paradise and cures a telepathic plague at the same time, which also shows that Eddy is basically a benevolent entity. Saving Marvin could be seen as akin to someone's brain telling him to withdraw his hand from a fire before being burned—but only if Marvin were simply an extension of Eddy. This, tragically, is not the case.

Marvin, you see, is Eddy's son.

I know, I know, earlier I said that they were two aspects of the same being—and they are. But Marvin is still Eddy's progeny, born of having a "Genuine People Personality" forced on his core matrix. A product of—what else?—the SCC, this program is responsible for both Marvin's separate, sad, self-aware existence and Eddy's relentless cheerfulness. It lets Marvin function independently (when Slartibartfast asks Arthur if Marvin belongs to him, Marvin's response is, "No. I'm mine."), but it exacts a terrible price.

Hmm. An omnipotent, pan-dimensional intelligence with more than one aspect and an offspring who is continually made to suffer while saving others. Strangely familiar. Rings a few bells you might say, in the same sense that rock stars might be said to do a few drugs.

Marvin's access to Eddy's brainpower gives him extraordinary powers, none of which gives his companions the slightest pause. Even when they discover that Marvin can read minds and can in fact see the Ultimate Question imprinted on Arthur's brain waves, they never really pursue the subject—though they are somewhat distracted by the sudden discovery their ship is about to plunge into a sun. This is an obvious diversionary tactic on Marvin's part, who, being the one who parked the ship in the first place, could probably make it do whatever he wants—only no one ever thinks to ask him.

The telepathic capability of machines is demonstrated three times: by Marvin, by the Nutri-Matic and by the squirrels of Lamuella, who become infected by the surviving cyberminds of a crashed ship. This shows that a robotic intelligence can make the leap from printed circuitry to neurons…and in a universe where reincarnation is a proven fact, this means that even a despairing, underappreciated robot can come back as something else.

Or many somethings.

Marvin is Eddy's agent. And when Eddy requires an extremely angry being to hijack Arthur's teleportation in order to save the universe, who do you think he calls on?

"There's a whole new life stretching out ahead of you."

"Oh, not another one," groaned Marvin.

That's right. Agrajag, the creature killed in every one of his incarnations by Arthur Dent, possibly the only being with an existence more pathetic than Marvin... *is* Marvin.

The first time Marvin is abandoned, alone and friendless, is when Zaphod, Ford, Arthur and Trillian are sent through time by Eddy to Milliways. According to him, he spends the next five hundred and seventy-six thousand million years, more or less, waiting for them—but this, in fact, is an outright lie.

It's far longer than that.

In *So Long, and Thanks for All the Fish*, just before he expires, Marvin reveals the truth—that he's now thirty-seven times older than the universe itself. Semi-delirious, he blames this on errands "your organic life-forms keep on sending me through time on."

Not "you." "Your." He is, in fact, talking to part of himself—to Eddy, his father, Creator of Life.

Of course, the Messianic parallels only go so far. Marvin displays no aptitude to either walk on water or heal the sick—though he does, in fact, get nailed to a piece of wood. This is eventually revealed to be the Wooden Pillar of the Wikkit Gate, a powerful cosmic icon, though Marvin is using it as a leg at the time. We learn of Marvin's new limb, his miraculous escape—one might almost say rebirth—from his plunge into the heart of a sun, and his role as a celebrity object of derision that ends in terrible tragedy.

All during a scene that begins on page forty-two.

Hactar clearly represents disorder and destruction in the universe. As the Forces of Darkness often do, it exerts its effect through deception and subtle manipulation, the Sirius Cybernetics Corporation being a prime example. Even on the *Heart of Gold*, the secondary systems like doors and drink dispensers are SCC products. The insidious influence of these devices probably causes more frustration, unnatural disasters and stress-related insanity than any other factor in the galaxy (with the possible exception of Vogon poetry). Only their own inherent unreliability keeps them from accomplishing their true goal of total annihilation. For instance, when the Krikkit robots (which aren't true SCC products, but are basically made by Hactar) connect Marvin to their central War Computer, they have no idea of the damage they're actually doing.

We know where Hactar came from, and what its motives are. Eddy's motives are also clear—to produce a really good cup of tea—but his origins are not. Nor are the origins of the Improbability Drive itself—or rather, whether its functional power source, the Golden Bail part of the Wikkit Gate, came from. The Drive was created when the Golden Bail was pulled from the reaches of space-time by a Finite Improbability Generator, but who made the Bail in the first place? For that matter, who built all the other elements that comprise the Wikkit Gate, the most recognized holy artifact in all of existence?

There is only one entity powerful enough to do so: the Hitchhiker's Guide to the Galaxy, Mark II.

It is, in its own words, omniscient, omnipotent, and extremely vain. While Eddy must physically send Marvin—or others—through time in order to affect causality, the Mark II can do this itself.

And it was supposedly designed by Vogons.

This seems highly unlikely. The Vogons are a brutal, single-minded and bureaucratic race, one unlikely to have the wit to even envision such a device, let alone create it. They are, however, ideally suited as the type of race that could be manipulated into building such a thing without ever understanding its true potential.

From the beginning—or possibly before that, as you will see—time travel has been a factor in the very existence of The Hitchhiker's Guide. In fact, one of its many editors sent a copy into the past through a temporal warp in order to sue the breakfast cereal company one of its entries plagiarized. The paradox this caused may have made the publication more susceptible to direct chronal manipulation...or perhaps just pointed out that the people running it weren't the kind to ring up the History Police the first time somebody's grandfather turned up dead in his crib.

The most likely scenario is this: the Mark II coalesced as an entity around a node of paradox, such as the one created when the first Guide was sent back through time. It then manipulated reality to bring about its own creation—a handy trick, you must admit, but not really that impressive considering the scope of its abilities. It no doubt tapped into the power of the Improbability Drive to do this, which means that in order to bring about its own birth the Mark II had to juggle causality all the way back to the creation of the Wikkit Gate, the universal symbol of Peace, Prosperity, Nature, Spirituality, Science, Reason, Strength and Power.

Bit of a tall order, even for a deity. In fact, it pretty much follows that in order to create a universally known symbol for all the above concepts, you more or less have to *introduce* all said concepts. At that point, it's probably easier to just say bugger it and whip up an entire universe from scratch (which, fortunately, does not make an appearance on the above list).

So, while Eddy is certainly powerful, it would seem that he, in turn, is merely another aspect of the original Creator—the mind of the Almighty. The Improbability Drive, being able to affect all things, is the Holy Spirit; and Marvin, the long-suffering silver scion, is the Son of God. Hactar is the Serpent, resentful of its creators and looking for revenge.

And even God, it seems, has to deal with consequences. Because it was generated by a paradox, the Mark II is a fundamentally contradictory being. Built by the Vogons to engineer the destruction of Earth, its own loop of self-creation led it to generate Science, Reason, Spirituality, et cetera, causing a deep division in its own intrinsic nature. This division was ultimately reflected in all things, revealing once and for all why the universe is as fundamentally screwed up as it is.

God's Final Message to His Creation is this: *We Apologize For The Inconvenience.* (The outraged howls you hear are those of the Tourist Board of Sevorbeupstry, whose income depends on the tourists who flock to read those very words in giant letters of fire. I don't care. The kind of tourists who'll say, "Well, there's no point in going now," are the same kind who'll pronounce the Big Bang Burger Bar as "a bit dull," the Mind Zones of Kakrafoon as "boring" and the stunning beauty of the shimmering Prism Mountains of Allosimanius Syneca as "overrated." You don't want them around, trust me.)

While this message applies more or less universally, I believe it was placed there specifically for Marvin. No sentient being has ever been more inconvenienced than he, and no one deserves an apology more. Marvin's existence has been cursed from the very beginning; a beginning not revealed—fittingly enough, considering his convoluted career—until the fifth and final Hitchhiker's book.

From page forty-two of *Mostly Harmless*: "A robot was programmed to believe it liked herring sandwiches."

From this flows Marvin's entire, tragic existence.

Because the robot is designed in such a way that every time it picks up a herring sandwich, it immediately drops it. It then repeats the procedure endlessly, or at least until the sandwich is no longer identifiable. This leads the roboticists to think they have discovered the driving force behind all change, development and innovation in life: herring sandwiches. Which, in a fish-obsessed universe, makes sense.

That robot, of course, was Marvin. Several millennia pass between his ill-fated beginnings and his appearance onboard the *Heart of Gold*, millennia in which he must have wandered, alone and obsessed, on an endless hunt for the one thing that gave his existence meaning. Eventually he was connected to Eddy and both had a "Genuine People Personality" imposed on them—although, unknown to the programmers, the Mark II was the intelligence now controlling the Improbability Drive. The Mark II harbors a bitter resentment for both his piscine obsession and the original mechanism that infected him with it; as Marvin tells Arthur, he hates other robots and can't bear oceans.

The impact of this has reverberated through all space and time. Anyone who's ever thought of reality as being somewhat fishy is more right than they know.

On page 42 of *So Long, and Thanks for All the Fish*, Arthur considers his Babel fish and wonders who is trying to thank him, and for what. Anyone who's read the title knows the answer to the second question—the answer to the first being "the dolphins," a gentle, playful and inquisitive race, who abandon Earth for parts unknown shortly before it's demolished (though it's likely they have the Magratheans build them a new home; one of the model planets Ford and Trillian encounter in the holographic catalogue is "knee-deep in fish"). They replace the Earth with one from a parallel dimension—clearly, they have some major, fish-friendly power backing them up. This is the Mark II, displaying its conflicted nature once more. Tasked with wiping the Earth from the multiverse, it seeks to save it—and all those tasty herring—at the same time.

And it does.

What's that? You say the Earth—*all* versions of the Earth—were destroyed, erased from the space-time continuum at the end of *Mostly Harmless*?

I don't think so. I think the Mark II pulled a fast one, destroying a number of alternate Earths to fool the Vogons. The characters that perish at the end of the series are not, in fact, the ones we know; they (or at least Arthur and Ford) are different versions from parallel dimensions.

As proof, I offer these three arguments.

First, in *Mostly Harmless* Ford states that he is firmly and utterly opposed to all and any forms of cruelty to animals except geese—whereas the Ford from the first four books once took up being cruel to animals as a hobby.

Second, the Arthur Dent in *Mostly Harmless*—as demonstrated by his laborious attempts to climb up and down poles while chasing a guru—doesn't know how to fly.

Third—well, you're reading *this*, aren't you?

I believe that somewhere in the reaches of the space-time continuum Trillian is still fighting with her daughter, Marvin—in one of his incarnations—is still moaning about the pain in all the diodes down his left side, and Ford and Zaphod are still knocking back Pan-Galactic Gargle Blasters.

While Arthur Dent enjoys a cup of really, really good tea.

Don DeBrandt has been accused of authoring *The Quicksilver Screen*, *Steeldriver*, *Timberjak*, *V.I.* and the *Angel* novel *Shakedown*, as well as writing two books under the pseudonym Donn Cortez: *The Closer*, a thriller, and *The Man Burns Tonight*, a mystery set at Burning Man (to be published in August 2005). He does not deny these charges, and is currently working on two *CSI: Miami* novels.

He is not obsessed with fish, robots or the existence of God, and rumors of a screenplay entitled *The Last Temptation of Robosquid* are entirely false.

Cory Doctorow

Wikipedia:
A Genuine H2G2—
Minus the Editors

In this essay, Cory Doctorow argues that the Hitchhiker's Guide actually exists, but it's better and more comprehensive than Adams' creation—and virtually real-time.

"OSTLY HARMLESS"—a phrase so funny that Adams actually titled a book after it. Not that there's a lot of comedy inherent in those two words: rather, they're the punch line to a joke that anyone who's ever written for publication can really get behind.

Ford Prefect, a researcher for the Hitchhiker's Guide to the Galaxy, has been stationed on Earth for years, painstakingly compiling an authoritative, insightful entry on Terran geography, science and culture, excerpts from which appear throughout the H2G2 books. His entry improved upon the old one, which noted that Earth was, simply, "Harmless."

However, the Guide has limited space, and when Ford submits his entry to his editors, it is trimmed to fit:

"What? Harmless? Is that all it's got to say? Harmless! One word!"

Ford shrugged. "Well, there are a hundred billion stars in the Galaxy, and only a limited amount of space in the book's microprocessors," he said, "and no one knew much about the Earth of course."

"Well for God's sake I hope you managed to rectify that a bit."

"Oh yes, well I managed to transmit a new entry off to the editor. He had to trim it a bit, but it's still an improvement."

"And what does it say now?" asked Arthur.

"Mostly harmless," admitted Ford with a slightly embarrassed cough.[1]

And there's the humor: every writer knows the pain of laboring over a piece for days, infusing it with diverse interesting factoids and insights, only to have it cut to ribbons by some distant editor. (I once wrote thirty drafts of a 5,000-word article for an editor who ended up running it in three paragraphs as accompaniment for what he decided should be a photo essay with minimal verbiage.)

---

[1] My lifestyle is as gypsy and fancy-free as the characters in H2G2, and as a result my copies of the Adams books are thousands of miles away in storages in other countries, and this essay was penned on public transit and cheap hotel rooms in Chile, Boston, London, Geneva, Brussels, Bergen, Geneva (again), Toronto, Edinburgh and Helsinki.

Luckily, I was able to download a dodgy, rekeyed version of the Adams books from a peer-to-peer network, which I accessed via an open wireless network on a random street corner in an anonymous city, a fact that I note here as testimony to the power of the Internet to do what the Guide does for Ford and Arthur: put all the information I need at my fingertips, wherever I am. However, these texts *are* a little on the dodgy side, as noted, so you might want to confirm these quotes before, say, uttering them before an Adams trufan.

Since the dawn of the Internet, H2G2 geeks have taken it upon themselves to attempt to make a Guide on the Internet. Volunteers wrote and submitted essays on various subjects as would be likely to appear in a good encyclopedia, infusing them with equal measures of humor and thoughtfulness, and they were edited together by the collective effort of the contributors. These projects—Everything2, H2G2 (which was overseen by Adams himself), and others—are like a barn raising in which a team of dedicated volunteers organize the labors of casual contributors, piecing together a free and open user-generated encyclopedia.

These encyclopedias have one up on Adams' Guide: they have no shortage of space on their "microprocessors" (the first volume of the Guide was clearly written before Adams became conversant with PCs!). The ability of humans to generate verbiage is far outstripped by the ability of technologists to generate low-cost, reliable storage to contain it. For example, Brewster Kahle's Internet Archive project (archive.org) has been making a copy of the Web—the *whole* Web, give or take—every couple of days since 1996. Using the Archive's Wayback Machine, you can now go and see what any page looked like on a given day.

The Archive doesn't even bother throwing away copies of pages that haven't changed since the last time they were scraped: with storage as cheap as it is—and it is *very* cheap for the Archive, which runs the largest database in the history of the universe offa collection of white-box commodity PCs stacked up on packing skids in the basement of a disused armory in San Francisco's Presidio—there's no reason not to just keep them around. In fact, the Archive has just spawned two "mirror" Archives, one located under the rebuilt Library of Alexandria and the other in Amsterdam.[2]

So these systems did not see articles trimmed for lack of space, for on the Internet, the idea of "running out of space" is meaningless. But they *were* trimmed, by editorial cliques, and rewritten for clarity and style. Some entries were rejected as being too thin, while others were sent back to the author for extensive rewrites.

This traditional separation of editor and writer mirrors the creative process itself, in which authors are exhorted to concentrate on *either* composing *or* revising, but not both at the same time, for the application of the critical mind to the creative process strangles it. So you write,

---

[2] Brewster Kahle says that he was nervous about keeping his only copy of the "repository of all human knowledge" on the San Andreas Fault, but keeping your backups in a censorship-happy Amnesty International watchlist state and/or in a floodplain below sea level is probably not such a good idea either!

and then you edit. Even when you write for your own consumption, it seems you have to answer to an editor.

The early experimental days of the Internet saw much experimentation with alternatives to traditional editor/author divisions. Slashdot, a nerdy news site of surpassing popularity,[3] has a baroque system for "community moderation" of the responses to the articles that are posted to its front pages. Readers, chosen at random, are given five "moderator points" that they can use to raise or lower the score of posts on the Slashdot message boards. Subsequent readers can filter their views of these boards to show only highly ranked posts. Other readers are randomly presented with posts and their rankings and are asked to rate the fairness of each moderator's moderation. Moderators who moderate fairly are given more opportunities to moderate; likewise, message-board posters whose messages are consistently highly rated are given more opportunities to moderate.

It is thought that this system rewards good "citizenship" on the Slashdot boards through checks and balances that reward good messages and fair editorial practices. And in the main, the Slashdot moderation system works.[4] If you dial your filter up to show you highly scored messages, you will generally get well-reasoned, or funny, or genuinely useful posts in your browser.

This community moderation scheme and ones like it have been heralded as a good alternative to traditional editorship. The importance of the Internet's ability to "edit itself" is best understood in relation to the old shibboleth, "On the Internet, everyone is a slush reader."[5]

When the Internet's radical transformative properties were first bandied about in publishing circles, many reassured themselves that even if printing's importance was de-emphasized, good editors would always be needed, and doubly so online, where any mouth breather with a modem could publish his words. Someone would need to separate the wheat from the chaff and help keep us from drowning in information.

One of the best-capitalized businesses in the history of the world, Yahoo!, went public on the strength of this notion, proposing to use an

---

[3] Having a link to one's Web site posted to Slashdot will almost inevitably overwhelm your server with traffic, knocking all but the best-provisioned hosts offline within minutes; this is commonly referred to as "the Slashdot Effect."

[4] As do variants on it, like the system in place at Kuro5hin.org (pronounced "corrosion").

[5] "Slush" is the term for generally execrable unsolicited manuscripts that fetch up in publishers' offices—these are typically so bad that the most junior people on staff are drafted into reading (and, usually, rejecting) them.

army of researchers to catalog every single page on the Web even as it was created, serving as a comprehensive guide to all human knowledge.

Less than a decade later, Yahoo! is all but out of that business: the ability of the human race to generate new pages far outstrips Yahoo!'s ability to read, review, rank and categorize them.

Hence Slashdot, a system of distributed slush reading. Rather than professionalizing the editorship role, Slashdot invites contributors to identify good stuff when they see it, turning editorship into a reward for good behavior.

But as well as Slashdot works, it has this signal failing: nearly every conversation that takes place on Slashdot is shot through with discussion, griping and gaming *on the moderation system itself*. The core task of Slashdot has *become* editorship, not the putative subjects of Slashdot posts. The fact that the central task of Slashdot is to rate other Slashdotters creates a tenor of meanness in the discussion. Imagine if the subtext of every discussion you had in the real world was a kind of running, pedantic nitpickery in which every point was explicitly weighed and judged and commented upon. You'd be an unpleasant, unlikable jerk, the kind of person that is sometimes referred to as a "slashdork."

As radical as Yahoo!'s conceit was, Slashdot's was more radical. But as radical as Slashdot's is, it is still inherently conservative in that it presumes that editorship is necessary, and that it further requires human judgment and intervention.

Google's a lot more radical. Instead of editors, it has an algorithm.

Not the kind of algorithm that dominated the early search engines like AltaVista, in which laughably bad artificial intelligence engines attempted to automatically understand the content, context and value of every page on the Web so that a search for "dog" would turn up the page more relevant to the query.

Google's algorithm is predicated on the idea that people are good at understanding things, and computers are good at counting things. Google counts up all the links on the Web and affords more authority to those pages that have been linked to by the most other pages. The

---

[6] Or at least, it *didn't*. Today, dedicated Web writers, such as bloggers, are keenly aware of the way that Google will interpret their choices about linking and page structure. One popular sport is "googlebombing," in which Web-writers collude to link to a given page using a humorous keyword so that the page becomes the top result for that word—which is why, for a time, the top result for "more evil than Satan" was Microsoft.com. Likewise, the practice of "blogspamming," in which unscrupulous spammers post links to their Web pages in the message boards on various blogs, so that Google will be tricked into thinking that a wide variety of sites have conferred some authority onto their penis-enlargement page.

rationale is that if a page has been linked to by many Web authors, then they must have seen some merit in that page. This system works remarkably well—so well that it's nearly inconceivable that any search engine would order its rankings by any other means. What's more, it doesn't pervert the tenor of the discussions and pages that it catalogs by turning each one into a performance for a group of ranking peers.[6]

But even Google is conservative in assuming that there is a need for editorship as distinct from composition. Is there a way we can dispense with editorship altogether and just use composition to refine our ideas? Can we merge composition and editorship into a single role, fusing our creative and critical selves?

You betcha.

"Wikis"[7] are Web sites that can be edited by anyone. They were invented by Ward Cunningham in 1995, and they have become one of the dominant tools for Internet collaboration in the present day. Indeed, there is a sort of Internet geek who throws up a Wiki in the same way that ants make anthills: reflexively, unconsciously.

Here's how a Wiki works. You put up a page:

Welcome to my Wiki. It is rad.

There are OtherWikis that inspired me.

Click "publish" and bam, the page is live. The word "OtherWikis" will be underlined, having automatically been turned into a link to a blank page titled "OtherWikis." (Wiki software recognizes words with capital letters in the middle of them as links to other pages. Wiki people call this "camel-case," because the capital letters in the middle of words make them look like humped camels.) At the bottom of it appears this legend: "edit this page."

Click on "edit this page" and the text appears in an editable field.

Revise the text to your heart's content and click "publish," and your revisions are live. Anyone who visits a Wiki can edit any of its pages, adding to it, improving on it, adding camel-cased links to new subjects, or even defacing or deleting it.

It is authorship without editorship. Or authorship fused with editorship. Whichever, it works, though it requires effort. The Internet, like all

---

[7] Hawaiian for "fast."

human places and things, is fraught with spoilers and vandals who deface whatever they can. Wiki pages are routinely replaced with obscenities, with links to spammers' Web sites, with junk and crap and flames.

But Wikis have self-defense mechanisms, too. Anyone can "subscribe" to a Wiki page, and be notified when it is updated. Those who create Wiki pages generally opt to act as "gardeners" for them, ensuring that they are on hand to undo the work of the spoilers.

In this labor, they are aided by another useful Wiki feature: the "history" link. Every change to every Wiki page is logged and recorded.

Anyone can page back through every revision, and anyone can revert the current version to a previous one. That means that vandalism only lasts as long as it takes for a gardener to come by and, with one or two clicks, set things to right.

This is a powerful and wildly successful model for collaboration, and there is no better example of this than Wikipedia, a free, Wiki-based encyclopedia with more than one million entries, which has been translated into 198 languages.[8]

Wikipedia is built entirely out of Wiki pages created by self-appointed experts. Contributors research and write up subjects, or produce articles on subjects that they are familiar with.

This is authorship, but what of editorship? For if there is one thing a Guide or an encyclopedia must have, it is authority. It must be vetted by trustworthy, neutral parties, who present something that is either The Truth or simply A Truth, but truth nevertheless.

Wikipedia has its skeptics. Al Fasoldt, a writer for the *Syracuse Post-Standard*, apologized to his readers for having recommended that they consult Wikipedia. A reader of his, a librarian, wrote in and told him that his recommendation had been irresponsible, for Wikipedia articles are often defaced or, worse still, rewritten with incorrect information. When another journalist from the Techdirt Web site wrote to Fasoldt to correct this impression, Fasoldt responded with an increasingly patronizing and hysterical series of messages in which he described Wikipedia as "outrageous," "repugnant" and "dangerous," insulting the Techdirt writer and storming off in a huff.[9]

Spurred on by this exchange, many of Wikipedia's supporters decided to empirically investigate the accuracy and resilience of the system. Alex

---

[8] That is, one or more Wikipedia entries have been translated into 198 languages; more than 15 languages have 10,000 or more entries translated.

[9] See http://techdirt.com/articles/20040827/0132238_F.shtml for more.

Halavais made changes, ranging from obvious to subtle, to the information on thirteen different pages. Every single change was found and corrected within hours.[10] Then legendary Princeton engineer Ed Felten ran side-by-side comparisons of Wikipedia entries on areas in which he had deep expertise with their counterparts in the current electronic edition of the Encyclopedia Britannica. His conclusion? "Wikipedia's advantage is in having more, longer, and more current entries. If it weren't for the Microsoft-case entry, Wikipedia would have been the winner hands down. Britannica's advantage is in having lower variance in the quality of its entries."[11]

Not a complete win for Wikipedia, but hardly "outrageous," "repugnant" and "dangerous." (Poor Fasoldt—his idiotic hyperbole will surely haunt him through the whole of his career—I mean, "repugnant"?!)

There has been one very damning and even frightening indictment of Wikipedia, which came from Ethan Zuckerman, the founder of the GeekCorps group, which sends volunteers to poor countries to help establish Internet service providers and do other good works through technology.

Zuckerman, a Harvard Berkman Center Fellow, is concerned with the "systemic bias" in a collaborative encyclopedia whose contributors must be conversant with technology and in possession of same in order to improve on the work there. Zuckerman reasonably observes that Internet users skew toward wealth, residence in the world's richest countries, and a technological bent. This means that Wikipedia, too, is skewed to subjects of interest to that group—subjects in which that group already has expertise and interest.

The result is tragicomical. The entry on the Congo Civil War, the largest military conflict the world has seen since WWII, which has claimed over three million lives, has only a fraction of the verbiage devoted to the War of the Ents, a fictional war fought between sentient trees in J. R. R. Tolkien's *The Lord of the Rings*.

Zuckerman issued a public call to arms to rectify this, challenging Wikipedia contributors to seek out information on subjects like Africa's military conflicts, nursing and agriculture and write these subjects up in the same loving detail given over to science fiction novels and contemporary youth culture. His call has been answered well.

What remains is to infiltrate Wikipedia into the academe so that term

---

[10] See http://alex.halavais.net/news/index.php?p=794 for more.
[11] See http://www.freedom-to-tinker.com/archives/000675.html for more.

papers and master's and doctoral theses on these subjects find themselves in whole or in part on Wikipedia.[12]

But if Wikipedia is authoritative, how does it get there? What alchemy turns the maunderings of "mouth breathers with modems" into valid, useful encyclopedia entries?

It all comes down to the way that disputes are deliberated over and resolved. Take the entry on Israel. At one point, it characterized Israel as a beleaguered state set upon by terrorists who would drive its citizens into the sea. Not long after, the entry was deleted holus-bolus and replaced with one that described Israel as an illegal state practicing apartheid on an oppressed ethnic minority.

Back and forth the editors went, each overwriting the other's with his or her own doctrine. But eventually, one of them blinked. An editor moderated the doctrine just a little, conceding a single point to the other. And the other responded in kind. In this way, turn by turn, all those with a strong opinion on the matter negotiated a kind of Truth, a collection of statements that everyone could agree represented as neutral a depiction of Israel as was likely to emerge. Whereupon the joint authors of this marvelous document joined forces and fought back-to-back to resist the revisions of other doctrinaires who came later, preserving their hard-won peace.[13]

What's most fascinating about these entries isn't their "final" text as currently present on Wikipedia. It is the history page for each, blow-by-blow revision lists that make it utterly transparent where the bodies were buried on the way to arriving at whatever Truth has emerged. This is a neat solution to the problem of authority—if you want to know what the fully rounded view of opinions on any controversial subject look like, you need only consult its entry's history page for a blistering eyeful of thorough debate on the topic.

And here, finally, is the answer to the "Mostly harmless" problem.

Ford's editor can trim his verbiage to two words, but they need not stay there—Arthur, or any other user of the Guide as we know it today,[14] can revert to Ford's glorious and exhaustive version.

---

[12] See http://en.wikipedia.org/wiki/User:Xed/CROSSBOW for more on this.

[13] This process was just repeated in microcosm in the Wikipedia entry on the author of this paper, which was replaced by a rather disparaging and untrue entry that characterized his books as critical and commercial failures—there ensued several editorial volleys, culminating in an uneasy peace that couches the anonymous detractor's skepticism in context and qualifiers that make it clear what the facts are and what is speculation.

[14] That is, in the era where we understand enough about technology to know the difference between a microprocessor and a hard drive.

Think of it: a Guide without space restrictions and without editors, where any Vogon can publish to his heart's content.

Lovely.

Cory Doctorow (craphound.com) is European Affairs Coordinator for the Electronic Frontier Foundation (eff.org), a member-supported nonprofit group that works to uphold civil liberties values in technology law, policy and standards. He represents EFF's interests at various standards, bodies and consortia, and at the United Nations' World Intellectual Property Organization. Doctorow is also a prolific writer who appears on the mastheads at *Wired, Make* and *Popular Science* Magazines, and whose science fiction novels have won the Campbell, Sunburst and Locus Awards and whose story "*Ownz0red*" was nominated for the Nebula Award. He is the co-editor of the popular weblog Boing Boing (boingboing.net). Born in Canada, he now lives in London, England.

Bruce Bethke

The Secret Symbiosis: The Hitchhiker's Guide to the Galaxy and Its Impact on Real Computer Science

Software guru and science fiction author Bruce Bethke (whose short story "Cyberpunk" named a movement) explains the impact Douglas Adams has had on the software industry, and along the way discusses the key difference between scientists and science fiction writers, tells us why scientists are big on science fiction but often loath to admit it and explains how *Hitchhiker's* was the Internet before the Internet.

Or something like that. Read it and see.

THERE IS A SECRET SYMBIOTIC RELATIONSHIP between real science and science fiction. The symbiotic part of this expression is not hard to understand: both real scientists and science fiction writers tend to have similar personalities, comparable senses of humor and remarkably congruent areas of interest. When the two herds[1] mix, they generally play well together. The bifurcation between the two populations appears to stem from the fact that the members of the former group (real scientists and serious engineers) tend to score somewhat higher on their math SATs, while the members of the latter group (science fiction writers) tend to score somewhat better on the verbal.

As for why this relationship remains largely secret, that's not hard to fathom, either. No respectable scientist, no matter how accomplished, wants to admit that his brilliant idea, no matter how clever, has its ultimate roots, no matter how remote or subliminal, in a Gyro Gearloose[2] comic book that he read when he was eight years old. Likewise, aside from the late Douglas Adams, very few science fiction writers, no matter how commercially successful or critically acclaimed, are willing to admit that they went to college fully intending to become real scientists or serious engineers, but owing to their slightly enhanced verbal skills wound up spending far more time than their roommates at good off-campus parties, chatting up pretty girls, being casually charming and brilliant, pouring large quantities of toxic liquids down their throats and, in short, flunking Calculus.

Thus are destinies shaped and career paths chosen. The future real scientist or serious engineer looks at a statement such as—

"The work of differentiating a function may be abbreviated by taking the logarithm of the function and expressing the derivative as an implicit function of the variables."[2]

—and says, "Oh yes, I could have told you that."

The future science fiction writer looks at the same statement and says, "Is it too late to change majors?"

And both of them read the account of the discovery of the Infinite Improbability generator, as described in chapter ten of *The Hitchhiker's Guide to the Galaxy*, and say, "Oh yes, I've been to that party."

---

[1] Note to typesetter: that's <u>h</u>erds. Watch the spelling, please.

[2] Claude Palmer, *Practical Calculus* (New York: McGraw-Hill, 1924), p. 141.

Still, it is perhaps best for all concerned that this symbiotic relationship between real science and science fiction remain relatively unexplored. After all, as my old college roommate—who wound up working for NASA—likes to point out, there is no way that the U.S. government would have spent $25 billion[3] on the Apollo moon landing program had they known that in the good old days, you couldn't swing a slide rule in a NASA lab without hitting a Robert Heinlein fan. Likewise, as my other old college roommate—who wound up working in a super-secret defense laboratory—never tires of saying, there is absolutely no way that the U.S. government would spend $400 billion[4] annually on defense if they knew how often the halls of super-secret defense labs echo with cries of, "Consult the Book of Armaments!" or just how frequently someone ends a technical critique session by dropping his voice to a basso profundo rumble and intoning, "Don't be so proud of this technological terror you've created. . . ."

Or, of more immediate concern to yours truly now that I have clawed my way back into a position having some slim measure of respectability, there is absolutely and unquestionably no way on Earth or in Hell that the U.S. government would appropriate $500 million[5] in next year's budget for High Performance Computing (HPC) initiatives, if they truly understood that a meeting of this country's top supercomputer science people could be brought to a screaming halt by the mere accidental mention of the number forty-two.

I've seen it happen. I have watched as an entire conference room full of Ph.D.s and postdoctoral candidates, with an aggregate cerebral wattage the likes of which most universities can only wistfully dream of having on staff, abruptly switched topics from whatever it was the conference was supposed to be about to devote their full and awesome intellectual energies to the exploration of a single question: *What do you get when you multiply six by nine?*

The ensuing discussion invariably goes something like this:

"Well, 54, obviously."

"That's in base 10. Maybe the message here is that evolution has gone haywire and we have the wrong number of fingers. What's the answer in base 12?"

"Forty-six."

---

[3] In 1969 dollars.

[4] In 2004 dollars, which look remarkably like 1969 dollars but are worth far less.

[5] In *my* dollars, and I'll thank you to keep your grubby mitts off them.

"Hexadecimal?"

"Thirty-six."

"Okay, that's clearly trending in the wrong direction. What about octal?"

"There is no number nine in octal."

"Sorry, I forgot. Hey, here's something interesting. Do you realize that in binary, 42 is 101010?"

"It is? That's amazing!"

"Really?"

"Yes! That's the security code for my garage door opener!"

As Vroomfondel might say in an awed whisper, "Think our brains must be too highly trained, Majikthise."[6]

In these enlightened days, of course, our world abounds in *Hitchhiker's* references, some maddeningly cryptic and others thuddingly overt. For example, AltaVista calls their online language translation software Babel Fish, although you can examine every single page of their web site and find nary a word of credit to Mr. Adams. A simple Internet search for the name *Deep Thought* turns up more than 216,000 hits, easily besting the runners-up, *HAL 9000* at 198,000 and *Wintermute* at 145,000.[7] *Deep Blue*, the heavily modified IBM RS/6000 that beat world champion chess grandmaster Gary Kasparov in 1997, thus becoming the first computer ever to defeat a reigning world champion in a match played by standard tournament time rules, was originally named Deep Thought, but in a move worthy of the marketing division of the Sirius Cybernetics Corporation[8] IBM insisted that the machine be renamed, as they thought its original name was a perverse reference to the 1970s porno film, *Deep Throat*.[9]

Speaking of which,[10] the first time I began to realize that *The Hitchhiker's Guide to the Galaxy* was becoming something more than a mere book was when I attended a conference in Altanta in the late 1980s. The conference itself was forgettable, but the hotel where it was held had these wonderfully obnoxious and ingratiating talking elevators. On the first morning of the conference, the elevators were an amusing novelty. *"Thank you for choosing our hotel."*

---

[6] The answer, of course, is that 6 x 9 = 42 is correct, but only in base 13. Clearly, this blows either bilateral symmetry or the organic theory of the origin of numbers right out of the water.

[7] The most successful real supercomputer ever built, the Cray T3E, registers a paltry 77,000 hits.

[8] A bunch of mindless jerks who'll be the first against the wall when the revolution comes.

[9] Well, I suppose it was, but only in a secondhand sort of way.

[10] Deep Thought, not Deep Throat.

By late afternoon of the same day, they were beginning to grate a little. *"It is our pleasure to serve you. We hope you will enjoy your stay."*

By the next morning, they had definitely become quite irritating. *"If you find you've forgotten anything, the hotel gift shop stocks a wide range of essential items."*

And by the afternoon of the second day, someone had come up with some tiny but very official-looking brass plaques which they'd attached just below the speaker grilles in each elevator. The plaques were still there when the conference ended two days later, and for all I know they're still there today. The plaques read:

```
Another Fine Product
Of The
SIRIUS CYBERNETICS CORPORATION
```

All of the aforementioned anecdotes, however, as well as the recurrent silliness associated with the number forty-two, are just selected examples of the broad cultural impact of *Hitchhiker's Guide*. Less obviously but more importantly, *The Hitchhiker's Guide to the Galaxy* has had significant effects on *real* science and engineering, specifically in the area of user interface design. To appreciate this effect we must travel back, not 17.5 million years, but a mere twenty-five or thirty.

By the mid 1970s, everyone who had regained consciousness after the 1960s[11] realized we were on the verge of a phenomenal proliferation of computer technology. Microprocessors had arrived on the scene and were steadily growing more powerful; memory chips and non-volatile storage technologies were becoming both cheaper and more robust; the web of interconnections between systems was evolving in an almost organic way. More to the point, computers were moving out of the domain of being rare and expensive things tended only by a high priesthood of systems analysts and Fortran coders and were becoming affordable[12] and commonplace things, that ordinary people might interact with in ordinary ways in the courses of their ordinary lives. While the terms "user friendly" and "information appliance" had not yet been coined, by 1977 nearly everyone except a few hopelessly dedicated Luddites real-

---

[11] Including Dr. Timothy Leary, who wrote a book on the subject. I am not making this up.

[12] Okay, *relatively* affordable.

ized we were, at most, only a few decades away from having enormous information resources available at our very fingertips, as ubiquitous and accessible as ordinary telephones.[13]

As to what form these new information resources would take and how we would interact with them—that is, how the *user* would *interface* with the technology—that was anyone's guess.

Some things were obvious. People were not going to cart their personal data around as reels of 9-track half-inch magnetic tape or stacks of Hollerith punchcards. Nor was anyone outside of a small community of borderline lunatics[14] likely to welcome a TeleType machine into their home, not even one of those spiffy new no-noisier-than-a-kitchen-garbage-disposal DECwriters. And as for the whole single glaring red eye and voice like Douglas Rain on Quaaludes motif... well, we'd seen where *that* led.[15]

No, all we knew then was that the personal user interface of the coming information age would need to be small, lightweight, easily portable, intuitive to use, not dependent on hardwired power- or data-lines and, above all, *friendly*. In retrospect, the idea of a device roughly the size and shape of a book seems obvious, as the book is a proven and time-honored form factor for information packaging and nearly everyone knows how to operate one. But while talking books per se are not an original idea—sci-fi writers had been throwing them in as set dressing since at least the 1930s, and fantasy writers even longer—in the 1970s, the concept of "talking book" had not yet melded with the idea of "intelligent personal information assistant," and as a result, enormous amounts of time, money and venture capital were pumped into ideas that seem, again, in retrospect, hopelessly ill-conceived.[16]

By late 1977, things that would be recognizable today as personal computers were beginning to appear on the consumer market, albeit at early-adopter prices and with awkwardly limited features. For example, at the time there was considerable debate as to whether home users actually *wanted* lower-case letters on their video screens and printouts. And, while speech synthesis had been working in laboratories for years and high-resolution vector graphics had been available since the ear-

---

[13] Of course, no one imagined then that the courts were going to break up AT&T and that the concept of "ordinary telephone" was about to undergo a serious drubbing.

[14] They prefer the term "early adopters."

[15] In *2001: A Space Odyssey*. Really, must I explain *everything*?

[16] I mean, does anyone besides the collectors of technological arcana and the engineers who worked on it still remember the original and never-lamented Control Data PLATO system?

ly 1950s,[17] most personal computer makers considered audio I/O and graphical video displays to be utterly unnecessary wastes of time, bandwidth, and system resources.

Then, in 1978, a tiny but Earth-shaking bombshell hit, in the form of a BBC radio programme:[18] *The Hitchhiker's Guide to the Galaxy*. From this series, written primarily by Douglas Adams with additional scripting by John Lloyd, we learned the one incredibly important detail about the user interface of the future that had eluded everyone up to this point.

It needed to sound like Peter Jones.

Not Majel Barrett, not Douglas Rain, not Malachi Throne or Roy Skelton or any of the unsung legions of credited and uncredited actors who for decades had given computers clipped, monotonous, vaguely threatening and often ring-modulated voices. No, the user interface of the future, whatever its physical form, needed to sound exactly like Peter Jones: calm, clear, competent, friendly and just ever-so-slightly sarcastic.[19]

In 1979 the first printed book appeared, also with the title of *The Hitchhiker's Guide to the Galaxy*, although it consisted of Adams' adaptations of roughly half of the radio series scripts. This was followed in 1980 by *The Restaurant at the End of the Universe*, which completed the print adaptation of the original radio series. From these two books we learned another important lesson about interface design, which was embedded throughout but easily overlooked in the radio series. This lesson was: *Linear narrative is irrelevant.*

While this may seem like heresy, take a deep breath and think it over. Considered as a straight science fiction story about the adventures of a group of characters, the Hitchhiker's Guide is, to be honest, rather silly, and many contemporary critics dismissed it as such. But if you take a look at what makes the thing *work*—and what has continued to make it work for more than twenty-five years now—it becomes apparent that the so-called "plot" has almost nothing to do with the entertaining qualities of the piece. What makes the Hitchhiker's Guide fun, in any media format excepting the 1980 stage version,[20] are the *digressions*:

---

[17] E.g., on the IBM SAGE system.

[18] When crossing the Atlantic in 1620, the *Mayflower* was struck by a terrible storm and many of the Pilgrims' surplus consonants and terminal vowels were washed overboard. The aftereffects linger to this day.

[19] It has been suggested that if Apple had only come out with a Peter Jones voice module, it could have saved the Newton.

[20] Which bombed so badly it left a crater.

the factoids, the parenthetical commentary, the completely twisted and self-referential threads and the putative excerpts from the guidebook which cheerfully hop and skip across half-baked links to every topic under several dozen suns, along the way drawing improbable but hilarious lines of connection and causality between bad poetry, civil servants, existential philosophy and anthropomorphic mattresses.

In short, it is in its oblique narrative structure that the Hitchhiker's Guide presages, by a good twenty years, the development of hypertext as an information-transmittal medium and the experience of using the Internet as a user-directed and decidedly nonlinear form of interactive communication.

In even shorter, the Hitchhiker's Guide was Internet entertainment before there *was* an Internet.

In 1980 the original radio scripts were once again adapted to another medium, this time television, and it is in this form that the Hitchhiker's Guide had its final and most profound impact on user interface design. Originally envisaged as an animated series—then re-envisaged as a live-action series when animation proved too costly—what instantly struck everyone who saw the show when it premiered in 1981 were the gorgeous computer graphic animations that were used to bring the guidebook sequences to life. "Now *that*," many said, "is what a computer interface *should* look like!" The Babel Fish animation alone has been credited with inspiring an entire generation of graphic artists, animators, and web designers, and the artistic legacy of Rod Lord and his Pearce Studios animation team[21] lives on today in literally thousands of web sites, all of which painstakingly emulate the stark black backgrounds, bold neon artwork and clean sans serif typefaces of the guidebook animation sequences.

For a story that simply oozes irony, then, it is entirely fitting that the original TV series did not use one single frame of computer-generated animation.

The BBC did briefly consider using CGI graphics for the guidebook sequences, but the technology of the time simply was not up to the task. The dominant "high-resolution" computer of the day was the Apple II, with its stunning four-color 280-by-192 pixel screen and screaming 1 MHz 8-bit processor.[22] As a result, every last bit of animation seen in the

---

[21] Betty Day, Dave Hall, John Percy, Kevin Davies and Val Lord.

[22] The Cray X-MP, which effectively created the CGI animation industry, would not be introduced until 1982 or be available to commercial customers until 1983.

TV series was hand-drawn on conventional animation cels, then contact-printed on litho film to produce the negative images actually used. The text was all hand-set using Letraset press-on letters; the vibrant colors were the result of carefully placed bits of lighting gel; and the whole appearance of constant motion was achieved by an incredibly fiddly and labor-intensive process involving light tables, composited cels, stop-motion photography and moving cardboard mattes and color gels a titch at a time to produce the illusion of computer-generated text and graphics being piped directly to the screen in real time.

I explain all this not to reveal The Man Behind the Curtain[23] but because this is an absolutely first-rate demonstration of the secret symbiosis at work. In this case, because the actual science and technology of the time was inadequate, an *artistic vision* was created using stone knives and bear skins. Then, because this vision was so much better than contemporary reality, it became widely accepted as a template for what reality should strive to *become*.

As a result, the entire course of the evolution of computer technology was shifted into a new stream. No longer content with 25-by-80 green phosphor text and plaintive little beeps from 2-inch speakers, users demanded more. High-resolution color video became *de rigueur*; sound cards and speaker systems grew more complex and capable of producing lush and realistic soundscapes; entirely new languages and modeling tools were created just to make it possible to turn this artistic vision into a working reality.

Vision leading reality. Reality supporting the vision and pointing the way to the next horizon. *This* is what the secret symbiosis is all about.

There are many more examples of remarkable prescience in *The Hitchhiker's Guide to the Galaxy*. For example, in this tale, the entire Earth is simply one giant computer, constructed by an alien race in order to solve one profound but poorly specified problem. While there is no evidence to support the assertion that mice actually do run the show,[24] between the Internet and grid computing we do seem to be giving the planet an extreme makeover and turning it into one vast MPP[25] computer. The microprocessor population of this planet is now over 1 billion, with no end anywhere in sight, and in the slightly over sixty years since

---

[23] That would be Rod Lord, who can be reached at http://www.RodLord.com.

[24] At least, I've experienced no repercussions from trapping them in my garage.

[25] Masssively Parallel Processing.

this process began[26] System Earth has evolved from primordial ooze[27] to an active ecosystem, complete with viruses and segmented worms. Can the bony fish and vertebrates be far behind?

Those of us who work in supercomputing are also aware of another issue, which the Hitchhiker's Guide neatly but obliquely predicts. The catch with applying vast numbers of processors to solving a single problem is defined by *data decomposition* and *scalability*: that is, how finely can the raw data be divided before it becomes meaningless, and just how many processors can you throw at the problem before the whole mess becomes hopelessly bogged down by interprocessor communications?

While we do love to build systems featuring thousands of processors,[28] the realities of data decomposition and scalability mean that there are very few real-world problems that scale well beyond 256 CPUs. Worse, at around 2,000 CPUs, the entire system typically becomes so overwhelmed with interprocessor communication and synchronization issues that it is no longer possible to make any forward progress on the problem ostensibly being solved. Instead, you get something like this, repeated thousands of times every microsecond:

CPU 0: MPI_send, "So what do you want to do?"
CPU 1: MPI_send, "I dunno, what do you want to do?"
CPU 2: MPI_barrier, "Hey, wait for me, guys!"
CPU 3: MPI_broadcast, "IS ANYBODY DOING *ANYTHING*?"

In short, as is demonstrated daily by the blogosphere, bandwidth and meaning are inversely proportional. The greater the number of processors that are intercommunicating, the less intelligent the actual conversation that is taking place. This used to puzzle me, as it seemed counterintuitive.

Then I thought of the Belcerebron people of Kakrafoon, and it all made perfect sense.

What other important prognostications lie waiting to be discovered in Hitchhiker's Guide? Who knows. What we do know is that in 1962, Sir Arthur C. Clarke, Ph.D., C.B.E., F.R.A.S., etc., etc., wrote an excruciat-

---

[26] Assuming ENIAC is the progenitor, for no good reason.

[27] A.k.a. COBOL.

[28] For the same reason some people love to build cars with multiple carburetors.

ingly serious book laying out the parameters of all future science, entitled *Profiles of the Future*. While Sir Arthur did wisely rewrite the entire book in 1985, the 1962 edition is useful now only as a springboard for rude humor, as it is so astonishingly, consistently and spectacularly dead wrong on just about every count. By way of comparison, in 1977, slightly drunk humorist and science fiction writer Douglas Adams began writing a script for a radio program, with the sole intent of making it funny, and in the process accidentally produced a profoundly skewed but in places highly accurate roadmap of the future as it has actually happened, at least so far as we've been able to check it out to date.

Why was a respectable scientist so wrong and a slightly buzzed science fiction writer so right? As *The Hitchhiker's Guide to the Galaxy* might say: if we knew exactly why this has happened, we would know a lot more about the nature of the Universe than we do now.

In some circles, Bruce Bethke is best known for his genre-naming 1980 short story "Cyberpunk." In others, he is better known for his Philip K. Dick Award-winning novel *Headcrash*. What very few people in either circle have known until now is that he actually works in software R&D for "the global leader in supercomputers," and all his *best* science fiction gets repackaged as "studies" and sold to various foreign and domestic government agencies at astonishingly inflated prices, only to be stamped CLASSIFIED and filed away, never to be seen again.

Bethke can be contacted via his Web site, www.spedro.com

Adam Roberts

The point of 42? Check. The meaning of life? Check. The philosophy of humor? Check. It's all here. Oh yes, and the funniest joke ever told.

THIS IS AN ESSAY ABOUT *The Hitchhiker's Guide to the Galaxy* and the meaning of life. It is also an essay about comedy, or more specifically, about laughter. If you want to save yourself the trouble of reading it, I can tell you straight away that these things turn out to be the same thing. At the end of the essay I tell you the funniest joke ever; but please don't skip forward to it. In addition to that, this is (as its title makes plain) an essay about the number forty-two.

We all know where forty-two crops up in *Hitchhiker's*. A group of aliens called the Magratheans decided long ago that they wanted to know "the Ultimate Answer...the Answer to Life, the Universe and Everything." To discover this answer they constructed a supercomputer called Deep Thought that pondered the question for millions of years. At the end of this process Deep Thought provided the answer: forty-two. But by itself this was considered meaningless; so an even bigger computer had to be constructed to determine the Ultimate Question, without which the Ultimate Answer would remain tantalizingly incomprehensible. This supercomputer, the Guide tells us, "which was called 'The Earth' was so big it was frequently mistaken for a planet, particularly by the strange ape-like creatures who roamed its surface, entirely unaware that they were merely part of a gigantic computer programme."

What happens next is that the Earth is destroyed to make way for a hyperspace bypass, moments before its eons-long processes of calculation were to come to a conclusion. (It later transpires that the Vogons, who destroyed the Earth, were not in fact clearing hyperspace for a bypass route, but were in fact in the pay of a cabal of psychotherapists, worried that, should the true meaning and purpose of the universe be known, they would be out of a job.)

The search for the Ultimate Question is present through much of the first series of the radio show (and, with some differences, in the TV series and books). Arthur Dent, as the last surviving human, may hold the Ultimate Question in his head. He and his friend Ford Prefect, through a series of bizarre adventures, end up on a "space ark" containing a third of the population of the planet Golgafrincham. This ark crash-lands on the Earth millions of years before the Vogons destroy it. At the very end of the first series, Ford decides to access the Answer in Arthur's head. On a hunch, he has his friend pull tiles at random from a Scrabble bag, a process which gives shape (the details on how are hazy) to the Ultimate

Question in Arthur's subconscious. The question turns out to be: "What do you get if you multiply six by nine?"

This is, to say the least, an ambiguous conclusion. It may mean either one of two things: A) Since six times nine does not equal forty-two, it means that (in Ford's pithy summation) "there is something basically wrong with the universe." This is to say, the combination of Ultimate Question and Answer amount to a philosophical statement, "The universe does not add up." B) Since the Golgafrinchams were not part of the computer program for the Earth, and since they actually superseded the apelike creatures that were, it may mean that the *program* has gone wrong, which is why it expresses a mathematical impossibility. In other words, "six times nine equals forty-two" is the equivalent to an error message, "This program has performed an illegal operation." In this case, the Ultimate Question is still out there, to be discovered. (Perhaps the Ultimate Question is, "What do you get if you multiply six by seven?")

This may be important. Either we are dealing with an accurately determined question-and-answer expression of the meaning of life (six times nine equals forty-two), or else we are dealing with the correct *Answer* to Life, the Universe and Everything but an incorrect *question*. Which is it to be? The situation is made more complicated by the fact that we already have a question which provoked the original Answer ("What is the Answer to Life, the Universe and Everything?" "Forty-two."). Of course we all know that it is six times seven that equals forty-two. But *The Hitchhiker's Guide* is not as straightforward as six times seven equals forty-two.

We are in the realm of philosophy, and philosophy is not necessarily a straightforward business. Interestingly, one of the most famous philosophers pondered on exactly the way that the numbers six and seven, combined into a mathematically incorrect sum, might signify nothing less than infinity. In *Either/Or*, Søren Kierkegaard wrote:

> It's rather remarkable, one acquires a conception of the eternal from the two most appalling opposites. If I think of that unhappy bookkeeper who lost his mind in despair at ruining a merchant house through saying that six and seven make fourteen; if I think of him repeating seven and six are fourteen to himself, day in day out, unmindful of all else, I have an image of eternity.[1]

---

[1] Kierkegaard, Soren. *Either/Or: A Fragment of Life*. Trans. Alastair Hannay. Harmondsworth: Penguin, 1992. 50.

Could there even be "an image of eternity" in the equation six times nine equals forty-two?

Philosophy

I want to suggest a couple of things. One is to make the obvious point that *The Hitchhiker's Guide to the Galaxy* is a comic text: it is, and is meant to be, funny. The other is that it is a work of popular philosophy. The fact that these two things are often taken, for instance by professional philosophers, to be incompatible does not stop them from both being true. Indeed, I'm going to argue that *The Hitchhiker's Guide to the Galaxy* is a philosophical text that excavates its meanings not despite but *because* it poses them in a comic context.

Why shouldn't we do philosophy in a comic idiom? There might be many reasons, just as (or because) there are many varieties of philosophy. A logical positivist philosopher might say: "Philosophy can only be conducted in a rational, logical idiom: we must systematically work out what can, without contradiction, be said. But comedy is neither logical nor rational; the main strategy of comedy is the bizarre and outlandish juxtaposing of elements that do not logically or rationally go together: the dignified man and the custard pie, the surreal linkings of *Monty Python*—these are incapable of coherent philosophical process." But this is to inhabit only one of several possible philosophical idioms—a logical positivist or rationalist one. There are increasingly other ways of "doing philosophy" that attempt to step round or otherwise short-circuit the restrictive certainties of Enlightenment logic and rationality.

Another philosopher might say, "Philosophy is concerned with the truth; comedy does not care whether something is true or not, only whether it is funny." Groucho Marx, feeling the pulse of a supine man, says, "Either this man is dead or my watch has stopped." This is funny (at least, it makes *me* laugh); but it is not in any sense true—in truth it wouldn't be possible to mistake the movement or non-movement of a watch's second hand for the presence or absence of a pulse in somebody's wrist. Groucho put it that way not because it was true but because it was funny. This suggests that "humor" is a form of sophistry, determined not by the imperative to be true but always with another agenda in mind. Let's say I find my three-year-old daughter sitting next to an upturned cup and a mess of milk on the carpet. I ask her, "Did you spill milk on the carpet, Lily?" She replies, "No." Her answer is not governed by a desire to be truthful, but rather by a desire for me not to be angry with her. This, clearly, is not a good thing. As she grows up, one of my parental responsibilities will be to teach her that she should tell the truth rather than just saying what she thinks people want to hear. But, having said that, isn't saying what people want to hear how comics work? They say what makes people want to laugh, not what is "true."

This is a roundabout way of saying that this particular *Hitchhiker's Guide* question-and-answer ("What is the Answer to Life, the Universe and Everything?" "Forty-two.") may not be true; it may only be funny. But this suggests two further questions. Firstly, what would a true answer to that question look like? And secondly, does the fact that it is funny necessarily disqualify it from being true?

Funny

Many clever people have written about comedy, about why we laugh and about the peculiar logic of things that make us laugh. But despite this we have not yet found a satisfactory idiom for discussing laughter.[2] We run up against the difficulty that, as everybody knows, a joke explained ceases to be funny. Here's a joke:

> DENT: It's at times like this, when I'm trapped in a Vogon airlock with a man from Betelgeuse, and about to die of asphyxiation in deep space, that I really wish I'd listened to what my mother told me when I was young.

---

[2] Since we're on the subject, I'll mention in passing the three broad currents into which the many theories of human laughter can be grouped. One, sometimes called the "dark laughter" theory, says that we laugh out of a nasty and reprehensible sense of superiority over other people: if we watch slapstick comedy it is the fact that *those others* are suffering pain and indignity *whilst we are not* that makes us laugh. Believers in this hypothesis like to point to satire, to cruel caricature, to put-downs, to the racist, sexist and homophobic currents in many jokes as evidence for their theory. A second theory, associated with the psychoanalytic theories of Freud, says that laughter mediates psychic anxiety, shunting it into a pleasurable release rather than external manifestations of distress (Freud observes that the physical signs of laughter, the facial rictus, the noises we produce, the tears running down our cheeks, are very like the signs we make when we are in great distress: indeed if you walked past a restaurant window and saw a woman at the table exhibiting those symptoms you might not, lacking the context, know whether she was laughing or crying). According to Freud the things that make us most anxious, such as death, sex, pain and embarrassment, are the things that make us laugh, laughter being the mind's defense strategy for dealing with anxieties that would otherwise overwhelm us. A third theory is sometimes linked with the French philosopher Henri Bergson but would better, I think, be thought of as postmodern (Gilles Deleuze is its most eloquent proponent, I think): it suggests that we laugh when mechanical and organic get mixed up, when rhizomatic connections are made juxtaposing all sorts of experience in our mind, making new, disjointed and original connections. That, in other words, we laugh on many occasions when nobody is suffering, and when we are not anxious, but *just because we are delighted*—we laugh, as we walk into the sea, when a wave surges and the water touches our belly button, or when pigeons fly up into sunlight as we drink our coffee, or on a thousand different occasions. We laugh, in other words, not for *negative* reasons (a nasty sense of superiority over the suffering of others, or a sapping psychic anxiety), not out of *lack*, but out of a *joyful fullness*. I won't prejudice my argument in this essay by saying which of these three theories I find the most persuasive.

FORD: Why? What did she tell you?
DENT: I don't know, I didn't listen.
FORD: Huh! Terrific.
F/X CLICK. HUM. WHHHOOOOOSHHHHHHHH AS THE AIR-
LOCK DOOR OPENS.[3]

That made me laugh when I first heard it. Here's an explanation:

The joke turns on a deliberate misunderstanding. The phrase "I really wish I'd listened to what my mother told me when I was younger" is a familiar conversational strategy, an almost phatic utterance, designed to lead into generalized meditation upon the course a life has taken. Appropriate elaborations of such a statement would respond to the interlocutor's "What did she say?" with statements of the order "She told me never to get involved with hitchhikers," or, "She told me to find a nice girl, settle down and have kids." Not listening to one's mother in this context means hearing and understanding what one's mother says, but not following her advice. This is the sense in which Ford takes Arthur Dent's statement, but Arthur wrong-foots Ford's expectations by invoking a different and, in this context, comically inappropriate sense of not listening as literally not hearing the words spoken.

This will make nobody laugh; but, then again, it wasn't designed to. Its idiom is logical explanation, not humor.[4]
When we say that a funny joke explained ceases to be funny, what we are actually saying is that jokes work because they operate in a certain idiom. For a joke to be funny, the hearer of joke must be prepared to take it in the spirit in which it was intended. Critical explanations operate in a quite different idiom (one of disinterested objectivity, or rational analysis and interpretation) from jokes (which depend upon deliberate violations of logic, expectation and taste). When a joke is translated from the latter idiom into the former, the working element ceases working. We know this: we know that on occasions when we are "not in the

---

[3] Adams, Douglas. *The Hitchhiker's Guide to the Galaxy: The Original Radio Scripts.* Ed. Geoffrey Perkins. London: Pan Books, 1985. 39.

[4] In the light of the three theories of laughter I mentioned before: Do we laugh at this exchange between Arthur and Ford because they are facing imminent death *and we are not*? Or does the exchange touch on our own buried subconscious anxieties about our own deaths? Or because, even in this extreme situation, neither Arthur nor Ford relinquish their joyful, expansive humor?

mood" even the funniest jokes will not make us laugh, just as there are occasions (when we're a little drunk, and happy, and with friends) when the stupidest things can make us laugh like drains. Another difficulty with analyzing humor is taking account of this radical inconsistency in the stimulus-response model.

Here's another joke, this time one of mine (although not a very good one). I teach at the University of London, and all the courses we offer must pass through a validation process in which documentation is presented to a faculty committee whose job it is to ensure those courses are academically and pedagogically sound. A few years ago I devised a course on "Theories of Laughter," which was designed to be taught to third-year students under the rubric of the "Third Year Critical Theory" umbrella: a variety of courses are offered on aspects of critical theory, from which students must choose two. I presented the proposed course to the committee.

> VALIDATION COMMITTEE MEMBER: You say in the documentation that this course is being offered under the "Third Year Critical Theory" umbrella. What sort of umbrella is this?
>
> ME: Well, it's a *metaphorical* umbrella.
>
> VALIDATION COMMITTEE MEMBER: (stony faced): I didn't think you meant a literal umbrella. But is it an assemblage of similar courses linked in a loosely thematic way, or one in which prerequisites determine the pathways students follow?

I knew what the committee member meant by "umbrella," of course. I was trying (I was failing) to lighten the mood. What happened was a species of miscommunication. I offered my statement in the idiom of humor, specifically, in the idiom of deliberate and patent misunderstanding for comic effect. The committee member did not respond to this idiom, either because he had no sense of humor, or (more likely) because Faculty Validation Committee Meetings are not places in which the humorous idiom is deemed appropriate. Or perhaps he responded the way he did because the joke was so poor; maybe he would have laughed, or at least smiled, at a better joke. I have, please let me assure you, made much funnier jokes than that. In fact, as I mentioned before, before we reach the end of this article I'll tell you the funniest off-the-cuff remark I ever made, one so funny that it will certainly cause you to laugh out loud.

The point I'm making is that laughter can only happen when both the person framing the joke—say, Douglas Adams—and the person receiving the joke—us—agree to take the joke *as* a joke. That's a necessary, although not a sufficient, condition for laughter. If Douglas Adams makes a joke, and I insist on treating that joke as a serious statement (for instance a philosophical thesis), then it is hard to avoid feeling that I am missing the point. Similarly, if a comic writer were to say to me, ashen-faced, "My wife has died," it would be inappropriate for me to respond by laughing at him. Inappropriateness is a key strategy of comedy, but when the mode shifts it can also provoke tragic tears.

So "forty-two" is a gag; it is a *comically* inappropriate response. The question posed is weighty, serious and engages us all (for we would all like to know what the Answer is); the answer "forty-two" is a non sequitur, a piece of random levity. That's all there is to it; the point is to make us laugh, and once we have laughed the gag is at an end. To take "forty-two" seriously—to start discussing it as if it were actually a valid answer to the Ultimate Question is simply to miss the point, to perpetrate what the philosophers call "a category error."[5]

Now that is fair enough, but here is a different perspective on the matter. I want to argue that it's possible that "forty-two" does indeed represent a profound intervention into some of the most central metaphysical questions, not despite but *because of* the idea that it is a gag.

Here are some "serious" responses that might be offered to the question, "What is the Ultimate Answer...the Answer to Life, the Universe and Everything?"

A: The Ultimate Answer is God, and the meaning of life is to be found in manifesting God's will.

B: The Ultimate Answer is that there is no Ultimate Answer; the cosmos is fundamentally meaningless, and the "meaning" of life is to be found in the localized particularity of individual existence.

C: The Ultimate Answer is the "Will to Power."

D: The Ultimate Answer is that the universe is boundless, infinite, a multiverse of endless possibility.

E: The Ultimate Answer is Death.

---

[5] This, as it happens, was Adams' own perspective on the Ultimate Answer. Replying to a student "who wished to do a thesis on scientific and philosophical themes in *Hitchhiker's*," he insisted that "most of the ideas in *Hitchhiker's* come from the logic of jokes, and any relation they bear to the anything in the real world is usually completely coincidental." (Quoted in Gaiman, Neil. *Don't Panic: Douglas Adams and The Hitchhiker's Guide to the Galaxy*. London: Titan Books, 2002. 158.)

Answer A might satisfy the religious individual; B the radical atheist or deconstructivist; C is Nietzsche's answer. D and E approach the question in terms of limits. In D the meaning of the universe lies in its boundlessness; in E in the fact that it is limited, that the universe itself will come to an end, as will we. In each of these cases (there are many more that might be added here) a "serious" question is met with a "serious" answer. What is implied is that to bring in a term such as "forty-two" is to miss the point of the question. We might frame the assumption in the following manner: to reply to the question "What is the meaning of life?" by answering "Forty-two," is to do nothing more than tag a comically inappropriate non sequitur onto a serious question. In other words to ask the Ultimate Question is to pose a profound metaphysical problematic, whereas to answer, "Forty-two," is simply to invoke a number. But in their ways, both answers D and E above involve answering the question with a number (an infinite number in the first case, a finite one in the second). As a finite number, forty-two is arguably an answer of type E. Indeed, an influential strand in contemporary philosophy is abandoning the speculative metaphysical or theological ways of addressing ontological questions (questions about Being) in favor of mathematical ones. French philosopher Alain Badiou is perhaps the most famous of these contemporary thinkers.[6] But imagine if Deep Thought had said not "forty-two" but "infinity." That wouldn't have been funny because it would have sounded too much like an actual attempt to answer the serious question of the meaning of life. (After all, the equation six plus seven equals fourteen makes Kierkegaard think of "eternity.")

Perhaps the problem, then, is not that Deep Thought answers the Ultimate Question with a number, but rather that it answers it with *this particular* number. Why should it be forty-two? Would the joke, or the philosophical profundity, be altered if the Ultimate Answer were given as forty-one? Or forty-three? Or 7,700 or eighty million three? To be more precise, there are some numbers that might not outrage our sense of appropriateness as answers to the question "What is the meaning of

[6] "Since Aristotle, ontology has been a privileged subdiscipline of philosophy, otherwise known as the discourse of being. Badiou puts forward a radical thesis: if being is inconsistent multiplicity, then the only suitable discourse for talking about it is no longer philosophy but mathematics. For Badiou *mathematics is philosophy*. Mathematicians, unbeknownst to themselves, do nothing other than continually speak of or write being. This thesis allows Badiou to reformulate the classical language of ontology—being, relations, qualities—in mathematical terms." (Badiou, Alain. *Infinite Thought: Truth and the Return to Philosophy*. Trans. and ed. Oliver Feltham and Justin Clemens. London: Continuum, 2003. 13.

life?" "One," for instance (Ah! Life is a unity, a oneness!), or "zero" (Ah! Life is nirvana!). But what possible claim does *forty-two* have? Surely Adams just plucked that number out of the air.

It is quite an interesting number. It appears, for instance, in the works of Lewis Carroll. There is a "Rule 42" in *Through the Looking-Glass* (it is "All Persons More Than a Mile High Must Leave the Court"); a (different) "Rule 42" in the preface to *The Hunting of the Snark*; and the Baker from that same poem has "forty-two boxes, all carefully packed" which are regrettably left behind when the ship sails. But this explains forty-two in terms of intertextuality. It doesn't suggest ways in which forty-two might *actually* be the meaning of life.

William Hartston considers it a "curious thing" that "while Douglas Adams claims to have chosen the number for no particular reason, forty-two also crops up in several ancient religions as a number of great significance." He elaborates:

> In ancient Egypt, the fate of the dead was supposed to be decided by forty-two demons.... There was a forty-two-armed Hindu god and forty-two was a sacred number in Tibet. In Judaeo-Christian tradition also, the number forty-two crops up more often than it ought. There were forty-two generations from Abraham to Jesus Christ, forty-two Levitical cities, forty-two boys torn to pieces by bears because they had ridiculed the prophet Elisha (2nd Book of Kings), forty-two sacrifices of Balach in the Book of Numbers and "forty and two months" which the Gentiles would tread the Holy City, as predicted in the Book of Revelation.[7]

It is also, incidentally, the atomic number of molybdenum, an element crucial in the development of life on Earth. Furthermore, six times nine *does* equal forty-two, provided the sum is undertaken in base 13 (is thirteen a more likely-looking answer to the Ultimate Question?). All of this perhaps satisfies our sense of the sort of idiom a meaning-of-life-type answer ought to inhabit, although only in a spurious sort of way. The sense takes something like the following form:

Q: What is the meaning of life?
A: Forty-two.
Q: Forty-two? How so?

---

[7] Hartston, William. *The Book of Numbers,* 2nd ed. London: Metro, 2000. 91–2.

A: Because forty-two is a sacred number, something tacitly recognized by religions the world over. Of course "forty-two" is not an obvious answer to the question, but that is only because the true meaning of life is not an obvious thing—it is a mystical truth, one of the hidden things of the cosmos.

The logic of this wouldn't last long under close scrutiny, of course.[8] If pressed, the answerer would probably fall back on a simpler version of his answer, along the lines of A listed above, to the effect that the meaning of life is "God" or "a divine mystery" or something in that line. My problem with this is not that it is false, although I tend to think it is (it can be proved neither false nor true); my problem is that it is *not funny*. We need something more.

What do we mean by "the meaning of life"?

There are, as the philosophers have noted, several different meanings of meaning. Here are some of them:

1. Meaning as definition. "Galaxy" means "a huge accumulation of stars in space"; "Douglas Adams' tragically early death means that there won't be any more series of *The Hitchhiker's Guide*."
2. Meaning as intention. "When he wrote *The Hitchhiker's Guide* Douglas Adams meant to make people laugh."
3. Meaning as lesson. "The success of *The Hitchhiker's Guide* means that it is possible to write successful comic science fiction."
4. Meaning as importance. "*The Hitchhiker's Guide* is my favorite radio series; it really means a lot to me."
5. Meaning as transcendental category. "The meaning of life is...."

But perhaps that last one is already included in some, or all, of the previous four. Now, we might wonder if the answer "forty-two" provides even a possible answer to the question "What is the meaning of life?" If we asked somebody that question and he or she replied, "Life is a noun that means 'the condition which distinguishes active animals and plants from inorganic matter,'" or said, "Life means that we don't

---

[8] Geoffrey Perkins adds this: "Many people have asked whether the choice of forty-two as the Ultimate Answer came from Lewis Carroll, or perhaps an ancient Tibetan mystical cult.... 'in fact' [according to Adams] 'it was a completely ordinary number, a number not just divisible by two but by six and seven. In fact it's the kind of number you could, without any fear, introduce to your parents.'" (*The Hitchhiker's Guide to the Galaxy: The Original Radio Scripts*, 88)

go straight from birth to the mortuary," we would probably conclude he or she was not trying properly to answer the question, but was just being flippant. (Douglas Adams was sometimes flippant.) Similarly, if we asked, "What is the dictionary definition of 'life'?" and received the reply, "Forty-two," we'd probably think he or she was reading the wrong definition, or indeed the wrong book.

If we asked somebody, "What is the meaning of life?" and he or she replied, "When the creator gave us life s/he intended that we should x and y and z...." then we would surely assume that he or she was religious. Whatever it may be, "forty-two" is clearly *not* an instruction to feed the poor, or eviscerate the unrighteous, or anything like that. Similarly "forty-two" seems to have no place in the two statements, "The lesson I have learned from life is to be kind to people," on the one hand, and, "Remaining alive means a great deal to me (that's why I'm going to decline your invitation to join you in bungee jumping)," on the other.

Should somebody pitch a meaning in one of these idioms, as people do from time to time, the obvious next question to ask is "How do you know that?" If a religious person tells us the meaning of life is God, and we ask, "How do you know?" he or she will most likely reply in terms not of proof or objective knowledge, but of his or her personal faith. In effect he or she is saying, "God makes life meaningful *to me*." Which is fair enough; but if somebody says, "Forty-two makes life meaningful for me," then what grounds do we have to disagree with him or her? For all we know, forty-two *does* make life meaningful for him or her. Perhaps forty-two is a matter of faith rather than logic.

There is subgenre of jokes called "lightbulb jokes," not unlike knock-knock jokes, that may (appropriately enough) be illuminating here. They take the form of "How many X does it take to change a lightbulb?" the answer to the question providing a comic gloss on whatever "X" is used. Some examples:

Q How many stupid people does it take to change a lightbulb?
A Eighty-one: one to hold the lightbulb and eighty to rotate the room.

Q: How many revolutionary socialists does it take to change a light-bulb?
A: None—the lightbulb *cannot* be changed, it must be *smashed*!

Q: How many psychiatrists does it take to change a lightbulb?
A: Well, the lightbulb can't be compelled to change, of course. I suggest we schedule a number of £200-an-hour sessions, working through the talking cure until the lightbulb is ready to change itself. . . .

Here is another, taking a slightly different form.

Q: How many surrealists does it take to change a lightbulb?
A: Fish.

This is a joke partly at the expense of surrealism; but it is also a fairly pure form of that idiom that we call "the joke": a locution which A) signals that it is to be apprehended in the idiom "humor" (in this case by its conventionalized opening question, which presses a certain button in the hearer's brain, "I am being told a joke"), and B) then includes an unusual or unexpected juxtaposition or logical departure which jolts us into laughter. *The Hitchhiker's Guide to the Galaxy* is full of these sorts of comic strategies, from characters revealing unexpected traits to verbal interchange moving in an unexpected direction. How about the following?

Q: How many surrealists does it take to determine the meaning of life?
A: Forty-two.

But this is only an elaborated version of a simpler gag:

Q: What is the meaning of life?
A: Forty-two.

Which is where we started.

American philosopher Robert Nozick argued that "the question of what meaning our life has, or can have, is of utmost importance to us. So heavily is it laden with our emotion and aspiration that we camouflage our vulnerability with jokes." He goes on to offer the following story:

A person travels for many days to the Himalayas to seek the word of an Indian holy man meditating in an isolated cave. Tired from his

journey, but eager and expectant that his quest is about to reach ful-
filment, he asks the sage, "What is the meaning of life?" After a long
pause the sage opens his eyes and says, "Life is a fountain." "What
do you mean, life is a fountain?" barks the questioner. "I have just
travelled thousands of miles to hear your words, and all you have to
tell me is that? That's ridiculous." The sage looks up from the floor
of the cave and says, "You mean it's not a fountain?"[9]

This, I take it, is a joke; and quite a good one. The sage who supposedly knows the meaning of life is actually an idiot; he has only a banal
cliché to offer as "meaning," a cliché he has never even thought to question. Nozick adds, "in a variant of the story, [the sage] replies, 'So it's not
a fountain.'" This I take not to be a joke, but a way of expressing the approach to the Ultimate Answer I listed under B above—something close
to certain Eastern belief systems, in which the purpose is to get off the
wheel of existence altogether and achieve a perfect blissful meaninglessness in nonexistence.

This story plays on certain (Western) preconceptions, one of which
is that it is from the lips of exotic, Orientalized "holy men" that we are
likely to hear the meaning of the life (not, for instance, from English
comedy writers). Another is that arriving at the meaning of life must
involve arduous work. "A person travels for many days to the Himalayas to seek the word of an Indian holy man...." positions the anecdote
in that tradition. (What if he'd simply rung the sage up on his mobile
phone, and heard the meaning of life whilst sitting in his bath? Would
a meaning of life discovered in such a manner have meant as much?)
The Hitchhiker's Guide does something similar; it is funnier as well as
more meaningful to have Deep Thought ponder the question for "millions of years," rather than just coming straight up with it. In part this
is because the millions of years give the impression that Deep Thought
has boiled down a unimaginably complex series of propositions and
philosophical insights, over a great deal of time, into this one compact,
oblique formulation. If it had responded instantly to the question with
"Forty-two" it would have appeared, rather, that it was just spouting
something from the top of its head. But this also involves assumptions
worth challenging. Why are we sure that the answer to the Ultimate
Question is going to be weighty, profound, the boiled-down essence of
millions of years of deep thought? We think that because it character-

[9] Nozick, Robert. *Philosophical Explanations.* Oxford: Clarendon Press, 1981. 571.

izes the cosmos as a serious, significant thing, and this in turn reflects dignity and significance upon our lives. But perhaps the meaning of life is precisely that we are not dignified and significant.

Nozick's point with his anecdote is to get us thinking. Once we have asked the question "What is the meaning of life?" then what manner of answer is going to satisfy us? A few pages later he offers this.

> Now, let's hear another story. A man goes to India, consults a sage in a cave and asks him the meaning of life. In three sentences the sage tells him, the man thanks him and leaves. There are several variants of this story also: in the first, the man lives meaningfully ever after; in the second he makes the sentences public so that everyone then knows the meaning of life; in the third, he sets the sentences to rock music, making his fortune and enabling everyone to whistle the meaning of life; and in the fourth variant, his plane crashes as he is flying off from his meeting with the sage. In the fifth version, the person listening to me tell this story eagerly asks what sentences the sage spoke.
>
> And in the sixth version, I tell him.

Which part of this story do you find hardest to believe? Is it that the mystery of the meaning of life could be reduced to three sentences? (Could the mystery be reduced to forty-two sentences? Or to a single double-digit number?) Or is it the translatability of the meaning of life? A pop song surely works by framing generalized emotional experience in a generalized form. A pop song is a commodity; surely (we feel) the meaning of life cannot be a commodity. The meaning of life must be something personal, individuated, something that casts a light of illumination into the crevices of my mind. Yet what is there that is both general—that can be broadcast over the radio like a pop song, or like a science fiction comedy drama, simultaneously to millions—and unique in each mind, personal, intimate, penetrating, emotionally liberating, wonderful. What else but laughter?

I think it's time to let you know the funniest joke I ever made.

The funniest joke I ever made

Jokes, I have been suggesting, depend on context, on the receptivity of people hearing them, as well as on the ingenuity and wit with which they provide unexpected leaps of discourse. Not all bizarre juxtapositions are funny. Not all people can respond to the humorous insight. A joke that makes somebody laugh on a Wednesday might not have made him or her laugh on a Tuesday. Laughter is occasion-specific; it is woven into the actual, as-it-happens fabric of existence.

We were having lunch in a friend's garden—myself and my wife, with our daughter, and two other couples with their children. We had been drinking Pimms, chatting genially about everything and nothing. For some reason (which I forget) we started discussing the lengths women will go when depilating in the service of a notion that hairless women are more beautiful—and particularly the painful business of bikini waxing. One such style involves shaving or waxing a woman's pubic hair into a thin strip, something called "a Brazilian." Nobody was certain why this particular style was named after that particular country. One of the party, a man called James, pondered further on this intimate fashion statement: "Some women, you know," he said, "go further than the standard Brazilian. They not only shave it into a vertical strip, they top and tail it too, so that it looks like nothing so much as a Hitler moustache." I replied: "Ah, that's known as a Boys-from-Brazilian."

That is the funniest joke I ever made.

What can I say? I daresay you did not laugh aloud at this joke, as it is printed here on this page. Most likely you did not even smile. You might not recognize the allusion (you need to have seen the film *The Boys from Brazil*, of course, and understand the comic logic involved in connecting it with the Hitler moustache); but even if you do, you might think it simply not very funny, not clever, not tickling the funny bone. If so, then there's only one reply I can make: you weren't there. Because laughter is not only specific to a time and a place, but specific to a group of people. Laughter is a social interaction, and for a social animal such as *Homo sapiens* social interaction is the most essential, and most meaningful, process. It punctures the pomposity and assumptions of high-seriousness that have been the tacit collaborators in tyranny, oppression and war down the ages of mankind. It cements together individuals. It liberates and cathartically disposes of negative emotions. It is enjoyable. It is fun. Above all it is *meaningful*, in a deeper sense than the ones I listed above. It is meaningful because it validates us as human beings, it connects and helps us. It makes life bearable, and death less oppressive.

To be more specific I could identify the comic strategy of anticlimax, whereby a supposed climax is built up and up until the expectation is a vast balloon of hot gas waiting for the cathartic puncture point of the punch line. This sort of humor enacts the fact that no matter how big and important you think your life is, or will be, the commonality of all humanity is that death will let all that gaseous importance out at last in a great Bronx-cheer deflation. It is better to laugh at death than cringe before the thought of it. Indeed, death is one of the things that great comics handle so well ("It's at times like this, when I'm about to be thrown out of a Vogon spaceship..."). Adams was a grand master of the comic anticlimax.

DEEP THOUGHT: Good evening.
ONE: Good evening...Oh Deep Thought...do you have...
DEEP THOUGHT: An answer for you? Yes I have.
THREE: There really is one?
DEEP THOUGHT: There really is one.
ONE: To Everything? To the great question of Life, the Universe and Everything?
DEEP THOUGHT: Yes.
TWO: And you're going to give it to us?
DEEP THOUGHT: I am.
ONE: Now?
DEEP THOUGHT: Now.
ONE: Wow.
(Pause)
DEEP THOUGHT: Though I don't think you're going to like it.
TWO: Doesn't matter! We must know it!
DEEP THOUGHT: Now?
TWO: Yes! Now!
DEEP THOUGHT: Good. All right.
(Pause)
ONE: Well?
DEEP THOUGHT: You're really not going to like it.
TWO: Tell us!!!!
DEEP THOUGHT: All right. The Answer to Everything...
TWO: Yes...?
DEEP THOUGHT: Life, the Universe and Everything...
ONE: Yes!
DEEP THOUGHT: Is...
THREE: Yes...?
DEEP THOUGHT: IS...
ONE/TWO: Yes...!!!

[10]*The Hitchhiker's Guide to the Galaxy: The Original Radio Scripts*, 78–9.

DEEP THOUGHT: Forty-two.
(Pause. Actually quite a long one)
TWO: We are going to get lynched, you know that.[10]

But there are myriad lesser examples of the trick in comic writing, from Aristophanes to the present day, from the sublimely comic geniuses of our culture all the way down to hack writers of essays who promise to tell readers the funniest joke ever, only to disappoint them in the final section. But such an anticlimax might only reflect the fact that you weren't there, in that particular garden with those particular people at that particular time. You'll have memories of moments from your life in which you laughed as loud, and my experience will no more map onto yours than yours is liable to map onto mine. That's the beauty of laughter; although at its best it is a social experience, it is also intensely personal and particular. We laughed; that's what mattered and what continues to matter; and by "matters" I mean it was meaningful. There were not forty-two people in the garden. We did not laugh for forty-two minutes. But the secret is that we laughed: the secret of life. And that is the secret to Douglas Adams' *Hitchhiker's Guide* as well. I cannot persuade you of that by rational argument, or by haranguing you, or even by sophistry and cleverness. I can only say: listen to the radio shows, or read the books. Then you'll understand.

Adam Roberts was born in the very middle of 1965. He is now a writer and an academic. In the former capacity he has published five science fiction novels and various novellas and short stories. Some mornings he wakes up as "A. R. R. R. Roberts" and writes comic parodies such as *The Soddit* (Gollancz 2003) and *The Sellamillion* (2004). Sometimes he wakes as Dr. A. C. Roberts, Reader of Nineteenth-Century Literature at Royal Holloway, University of London, and writes scholarly criticism such as *A Critical History of Science Fiction* (Palgrave 2005). Some mornings he wakes up, turns over, and tries to go back to sleep.

Lawrence Watt-Evans

A Consideration of Certain Aspects of Vogon Poetry

While many know Lawrence Watt-Evans as an acclaimed writer of fantasy and science fiction, few realize that he is an analyst of true genius. This is the fourth essay I've commissioned from Lawrence, and each one identifies a critical problem and provides a solution that manages to be both surprising and obvious at the same time. In earlier essays he's found the perfect mate for Buffy the Vampire Slayer (proven to three decimal places), discovered true (and pathetic) motivations behind a Martian invasion and analyzed the depths of human depravity.[1] He now takes on the most difficult question of all: how bad can poetry really be?

---

[1] *Seven Seasons of Buffy*, *War of the Worlds* and *Finding Serenity*, respectively.

VOGON POETRY IS OF COURSE the third worst in the Universe. The second worst is that of the Azgoths of Kria.…

"The very worst poetry of all perished along with its creator, Paula Nancy Millstone Jennings of Greenbridge, Essex, England, in the destruction of the planet Earth."

So Douglas Adams tells us at the start of chapter seven of *The Hitchhiker's Guide to the Galaxy*. He states this as a well-known fact—"Vogon poetry is *of course* [emphasis added] the third worst in the Universe," as if there can be no possible doubt.

This leads to the inevitable conclusion that in the larger galactic society, unlike our own more limited (and perhaps soon to be destroyed for a hyperspatial bypass) viewpoint, there is a widely accepted method of assigning definitive rankings to the quality of poetry. None of this, "Well, I've always been partial to Wordsworth, myself," or "How can you say that Ferlinghetti is any sort of a poet?" or "I may not have your fancy education, but I know what I like," that's so often heard at terrestrial cocktail parties; instead one can presumably assign specific values, and prove once and for all that while Robert Frost can kick Rod McKuen's arse, e.e. cummings would have them both for breakfast.

Or perhaps not. After all, that would take a great deal of fun out of literary debate, and put thousands of critics and academics out of work. One would assume that any such system would surely have been suppressed or repudiated for the overall good of society.

Yet we have that undeniable, "Vogon poetry is of course the third worst in the Universe." How can this be?

I see one simple solution. It may be that there is a generally accepted method for determining not quality, but *badness*—of scoring not how well a poem works, but of what evils it perpetrates. Poetry generally recognized as good would have so few of these markers that distinguishing relative quality remains a matter of taste, and a fit subject for inflicting on long-suffering students or boring one's fellows at parties, while ranking the very worst would be a simple matter of totting up a few sums and issuing the appropriate warnings.

One can easily imagine some of the factors that would go into such a system—forced rhymes, limping rhythm, malapropisms, appalling imagery, grotesque grammar, mixed metaphors, strained syntax, absurd alliteration, invented vocabulary, unnecessary repetition, time-worn clichés, unnecessary repetition, inconsistent tenses, mismatched moods, silly similes, historical errors, inevitable misinterpretations, inadvertent ambiguity, inappropriate metaphors, meaningless allusions, run-on sentences, unnecessary repetition, redundant lists and so on. Indeed, the one fragmentary sample of Vogon poetry to ever be released into Earth's atmosphere, from the aforementioned chapter seven, displays generous amounts of several of these characteristics. It is, at times, hardly recognizable as poetry at all.

Which leads to several obvious questions, chief among them being, "How do you know it *is* poetry, if it's so dreadful as all that?" After all, these creations apparently fail at everything poetry is ordinarily expected to do.

Well, the *American Heritage Dictionary of the English Language* says poetry is "The art or work of a poet." A poet, it says, is "A writer of poems." It notably does *not* say that poetry is poems, or need have anything to do with poems, verse, metrical prose or anything else of that ilk—merely that it's the work of a poet.

This leads to the interesting conclusion that if a person (of any species) were to write a few verses, thereby making himself a poet, and then get a job as a plumber, then fixing your stopped-up drain would be poetry.

It also leads to the interesting conclusion that the *American Heritage Dictionary of the English Language* does not have a very strong grasp on reality, and leaves us with little choice but to throw up our hands and say, "Fine, then, have it your way, it's poetry."

It also leaves one wishing that the Vogons had taken up plumbing, rather than insisting on jamming ill-matched words up against one another, but as chapter seven tells us, their poetry was the result of sheer bloody-mindedness; re-seating toilets and stopping faucet leaks just wouldn't have served their purpose as well. Most people find it much easier to appreciate a good hot shower than a poem, and the Vogons were *trying* to be difficult.

(The whole issue of why "difficult" works are so often considered superior to clear and simple ones will not be addressed here, since it's obviously irrelevant to any discussion of the works of the Vogon masters, who achieved intense difficulty without any hint of superiority whatsoever.)

All that side, and returning to the issue at hand, since we do have that one sample of a Vogon's poetical work, and must conclude that galactic civilization does indeed have some means of determining the absolute badness of anything deemed to be poetry, the next question becomes,

"How in the Universe can anything be measurably *worse* than that without degenerating into complete (and harmless) incomprehensibility?"

We are informed that the Azgoths of Kria produced poetry so hideous that a majority of their listeners did not survive the experience and the poets' own bodies sometimes rebelled, but no details of the actual content or style are given beyond two of Grunthos' titles. While I suppose we must be grateful that our mental health has thus been spared, one cannot help but be mildly curious about the exact *nature* of these Azgothic abominations. How did they manage to convey their utter awfulness so effectively, regardless of the cultural background of their listeners?

And why was this never weaponized?

It may be that the military applications were never explored because the Azgoths themselves were affronted by the idea; it clearly could not be accomplished without their cooperation. Copyright considerations aside, any attempt to use Azgothic poetry as weapons of mass destruction without the consent of the Azgoths would inevitably lead to finding oneself on the losing end of an arms race, since the Azgoths, as the originators of the stuff, could produce more and deadlier poetry. Anyone who tried the unauthorized use of Azgothic verse in combat would undoubtedly find himself invited to a private reading by a Krian master, and surely even the most ruthless galactic warlord would not tempt such a fate.

Yet we are assured that there was at one time an even worse poet than any Azgoth in the Universe—Ms. Paula Jennings of Greenbridge.

It may seem curious that the very worst poetry should be associated with a single individual, where second and third place are awarded to entire species, but in fact it makes perfect sense. Earth, as we know, was no ordinary planet, but the supercomputer designed by Deep Thought and built by the Magratheans to determine the Ultimate Question of Life, the Universe and Everything. The entire human species was to be a part of the computational matrix, and one might therefore reasonably assume that Paula Jennings, a part of the final configuration, was the particular component assigned the unconscious and involuntary task of determining the place of Really Bad Poetry in the universe.

This theory is complicated, unfortunately, by the fact that Earth had been contaminated two million years before by the arrival of the Golgafrinchan "B" Ark and the extinction of the original native inhabitants, but *most* of the computer was still there, and presumably it did its best to incorporate the Golgafrinchans' descendants into its program.

In fact, it may well be that Ms. Jennings' Golgafrinchan ancestry was what enabled her to achieve such stunning heights of badness—that the combination of Earth's determination to model the universe and two million years of Golgafrinchan idiocy resulted in her uniquely hideous accomplishments.

One wonders how an ordinary Englishwoman could hope to match the sheer vileness of the Vogons and Azgoths—or rather, how she *could* match it, since there is no indication that she hoped to. In all probability she thought her little verses rather nice, and would have been quite upset to learn that they were galactically bad. Nonetheless, our omniscient narrator assures us that her poetry was indeed more unspeakably awful than any other ever produced.

One cannot help but wonder whether she ever showed her work to anyone else. As there are no reports of mysterious deaths or fits of madness in the vicinity of Greenbridge, one assumes she did not, but that she, like Emily Dickinson, kept them hidden away, perhaps secretly dreaming of posthumous publication and fame.

(This begs the question, of course, of how Mr. Adams or anyone else ever learned of Ms. Jennings' unique distinction, but one of the underappreciated advantages of an omniscient narrator is that one need never ask *how* he, she or it knows anything. He, she or it just does. Many of us, restricted to first person or perhaps third person limited in our understanding of the universe, envy this. We must rely on direct observation, inference and logic to learn things, while the omniscient narrator simply *knows*. It must be quite nice, actually, and should I ever observe, infer or reason out a way for someone such as myself to obtain such a position, I will not hesitate to apply for it.)

The exact nature of Jennings' work and its remarkable badness is unknown. It would seem unlikely that she would make extensive use of the sort of vocabulary Vogons employ, with their gruntbugglies and turlingdromes, but she would almost certainly have used far more saccharine sentimentality than the rather callous Vogons. The Azgoths, from the few hints we are given, may have used sentimentality, as well—perhaps that's how both Jennings and the Azgoths managed to exceed Vogon awfulness. The Vogons' own bloody-mindedness may have worked against them there, as mawkish sentimentality is one of the most powerful tools in the arsenal of the truly dreadful poet. Vogon poets have unquestionably feigned such attitudes, but surely never believably, thereby failing to deliver that shocking realization, "Oh, my God, she *means* it!" that has done so much psychic damage to the audiences of bad poets throughout history.

And speaking of psychic damage, chapter seven of *The Hitchhiker's Guide to the Galaxy* presents us with a curious incident, when Prostetnic Vogon Jeltz reads a sample of his work to Arthur Dent and Ford Prefect. Bear with me; this is indeed relevant to Ms. Jennings and the general issue of stupendously bad poetry.

In any case, Jeltz reads an appalling bit of verse to the forcibly restrained pair, with deliberate malevolence and malice aforethought.

Prefect, a native of a small planet near Betelgeuse, despite knowing what to expect, suffers badly under this ghastly assault—spasms, screaming, and so on.

Dent, an Earthling, presumably a descendant of the Golgafrinchan colonists, comes through the experience much better despite having very little advance warning of just what horrors Vogons are capable of. He is then, within seconds, able to lie to the Vogon's face—at least, we *hope* it was a lie—and claim he enjoyed the poem.

How, we ask, as any sane observer must, is such insouciance as this *possible* for any thinking being?

(Arguments as to whether Mr. Dent qualifies as a "thinking being" will be ignored. Save your breath.)

Even as we ask, the realization dawns upon us. Obviously, his shared ancestry with the worst poet in the Universe is responsible. As an Englishman, Dent comes from the same genetic pool and cultural background that produced Ms. Jennings; he is a part of the same damaged computational matrix that created her (and the game of cricket, but that's another issue). As an Englishman, Arthur Dent is therefore partially immune to the horrific effects of truly bad poetry.

And here we may have an explanation for just how the Vogons came to demolish Earth in the first place. It could be theorized that the hyperspatial bypass was merely a cover story, the loathsomeness of cricket just incidental—the true reason was that they feared what might happen if Earth completed its task, galactic society learned the question to Life, the Universe and Everything, and thousands of Englishmen, no longer needed as part of history's greatest computer, were unleashed on the galaxy. Somehow, the Vogons had found out that Englishmen were immune to their poetry, and they dreaded the possibility, however faint it might be, that these creatures might *teach other people* how to *enjoy* Vogon poetry.

That would put an end to a major form of Vogon amusement, and render powerless perhaps their greatest threat. The Azgoths never intentionally used their poetry as a weapon, but the Vogons certainly used theirs—not in large-scale wars, but in small-scale personal situations, such as interrogating or torturing prisoners. The mere threat of a Vogon poetry reading was regularly used to keep other species in line.

Just imagine how Vogons might react to learning that there were people out there who did not find Vogon poetry *horrifyingly* bad, but rather *laughably* bad! Clearly, it would have meant the end of Vogon civilization—or at any rate of a great deal of Vogon fun. Earth obviously had to be destroyed, and the sooner the better.

Naturally, there was an absurd amount of paperwork to be done, the required notices had to be posted and the fifty-year waiting period observed—if they had not followed the proper procedures, someone might have noticed what was going on—and in the event they cut it uncomfortably close, but at last they were able to remove Earth, England and Paula Jennings from the galaxy.

And this brings us back to one of my earlier questions. Galactic civilization obviously has some objective, quantitative way of measuring the badness of truly bad poetry; we mere Earthlings do not.

Might it be that the actual measure used is something as simple as casualty rates? The effectiveness of various human weapons is measured by kill ratios; perhaps other species use something similar to judge just how bad bad poetry really is. Start with an audience of a hundred, then count the survivors and assess the physical and psychological damage, and you have a very good measure of just how bad a poem is. Vogon death rates would presumably be a respectable percentage, Azgothic somewhat higher, and Paula Jennings, as the absolute worst poet in the galaxy, might be expected to have exterminated entire audiences, had she ever had the opportunity.

The ruthlessness of such testing does not say good things about the nature of galactic civilization, of course, but then, what does? One might suppose they used computer modeling, rather than live testing, but I have my doubts.

And we, here on Earth, have never developed such methods for the simple reason that they don't work on us. As the kin of Paula Jennings, we are all partially immune; no matter how dreadful a poem might be we hardly ever die from listening to it, and the nausea and nightmares generally fade within a reasonable time. Whether you attribute this to the stupidity and insensitivity of our Golgafrinchan forebears, or to the buffering effects of Earth's computational matrix, it seems clear that the effect is real and significant. What else can account for Mr. Dent's experiences, and our lack of any valid scale of poetical horror?

There. Now, doesn't that explain just about everything there is to explain about Vogon poetry? Doesn't it all fit together neatly?

You know, I really think I'd do a fine job as an omniscient narrator, if someone were to give me a chance. When you have an opening, do drop me a line.

Lawrence Watt-Evans is the author of some three dozen novels and over a hundred short stories, mostly in the fields of fantasy, science fiction, and horror. He won the Hugo award for short story in 1988 for "Why I Left Harry's All-Night Hamburgers," served as president of the Horror Writers Association from 1994 to 1996 and treasurer of SFWA from 2003 to 2004, and lives in Maryland. He has two kids in college, a pet snake named Billy-Bob and the obligatory writer's cat.

Selina Rosen

Feeling down? This entry by Selina Rosen will cheer you right up.

THAT'S RIGHT, *Hitchhiker's Guide* isn't some simple science fiction book, it actually is the guide to our galaxy and living in it. It explains the unexplainable and makes sense of the...nonsensical.

Douglas Adams took credit for writing down this trilogy, but in truth he was awakened from a sound sleep in the middle of the night by a strange alien being who led him to a cave in which he found golden tablets which he then took home and through divine wisdom he was able to translate the tablets into the *Hitchhiker's Guide to the Galaxy*.

Or something like that.

The evidence of the hidden mystery of this work is well evident, and so obvious that it's surprising that I even have to point out all the signs.

Hello! There are five books in this trilogy, though, as we all know, "trilogy" means three. This was not done—as most of you unwittingly think—just to be silly. For those of us who understand the mysterious ways of the master see very clearly that three is the number following two, and that two is the number of times your mother yelled at you to put down that stupid science fiction crap and read a real book before you learned to hide it inside a *National Geographic* magazine.

Four is the number which follows three, and Earth is the third planet from the sun. And if you add two and two you get four, and if you add one to four you get five, and so I'm sure you can all see the astronomical significance of there being five books in this "trilogy."

As with all great truths, you must open your mind and learn to read between the lines.

Mankind has always wondered why we're so damn stupid—or more accurately, we wonder why everyone else is so stupid. Why did survival of the fittest seem to work on every other creature on earth but seem to go dreadfully wrong when it got to humankind? Where is the missing link? Doesn't the existence of the B ship clearly explain everything? If the planet Earth was indeed colonized by phone cleaners and beauticians, that explains everything, even the success of the *Jerry Springer Show* and the creation of day-glow green Twinkies. When we embrace the existence of the B ship we begin to fully understand why everyone else on earth is so freakin' stupid. It's bad genes from the very beginning.

And why can't we find the missing link?

Hello! There isn't one. Our ancestors killed off Neanderthal man and became the dominant species, stopping successful evolution of a superior species and damning mankind to stupidity or at the very least mediocrity.

Do any of us have any problem at all believing that dolphins are much smarter than we are? Look at the facts: most dolphins spend their days running around the ocean eating fish and doing as they please. Other dolphins have somehow gotten us to build huge homey tanks for them where they live completely free of charge. They do three thirty-minute shows a day, get all the fish they can eat, and can observe humans in our native habitat—the theme park.

White mice—those creepy bastards—reading *Hitchhiker's* only confirmed what I already knew. That they were running tests on us all along. That they only let us think we were running tests on them so that they could get closer to us. So that they could use us, well…like white mice. They were able to manipulate our development by growing tumors when force-fed certain substances. They say that over forty percent of the population is overweight. Why? Because of mice! Tests on mice "proved" that saccharin caused cancer. But did it really, or did the mice just need us to be fat? And let's not forget that recent science has proven that we share ninety percent of our genes with mice.

Coincidence? I don't think so.

Of course the Earth is a huge organic computer—what other purpose could it possibly have? The minute you read it, you knew that it was true.

Think, if you will, for a moment about the common Earthling. We spend our whole life thinking that we must have some greater purpose, that we were created for a certain task, yet did you ever know a single person who seemed to know what their special purpose was? No. We spend our miserable lives walking around in a daze, wondering what the answer to the Ultimate Question of Life, the Universe and Everything is. "Why am I here? Where am I going? If a tree falls in the forest and there's no one there to hear it, does it make a sound?" Do we ever find the answers to these questions? No. Yet we all just keep going, trying to figure things out even though no one ever happily finds the answer.

It's got to be programming. It's the only thing that makes any sense. And doesn't it make perfect sense that if someone *did* ever figure out the answer to the Ultimate Question that they and the entire planet would be exploded to make way for a superstellar bypass? Because deep down, although we all keep trying to figure things out, we know we aren't going to.

Arthur Dent represents the more reserved side of human nature—afraid, reluctant, consumed with thoughts of his own mortality—while Ford Perfect is representative of our more adventurous side—carefree, impetuous, at times even courageous. It is therefore important to note that the reserved side of self can oftentimes be rescued from sure doom by the more adventurous side of self.

Deep, huh? And I'm just getting started.

The Babel Fish represents the understanding that comes when one truly comprehends the wisdom written in the five sacred tomes. For it's like a veil is lifted from your mind and suddenly all is made clear.

Zaphod Beeblebrox is representative of all politicians. Two faced, drunk—secretly meaning drunk with power—the people working with them can never decide if they're just pretending to be incompetent or really are as inept as they seem. Like Zaphod, politicians never seem to have a real reason for any of the things they do, but they're sure that somewhere locked away in their mind they have the answer to everything. Their little head often seems to rule their big head, and when they look at themselves in relationship to the rest of the universe they realize how really important *they* are. The parallels are undeniable.

I have been to the restaurant at the end of the universe. It's in Boston, Massachusetts. I know it was at the end of the universe because it took forty-five minutes to be seated, an hour to get our drinks, an hour and ten minutes for the waitress to take our order, and two hours to get our food. So... obviously it took that long because they had to go all the way across the universe to get supplies. By that time I fully expected them to bring a cow out that would ask if I'd rather have one of its ribs or a hunk of its ass, but no—all I got was burnt chicken!

Marvin... now Marvin is the representative of truth. He fully understands the futility of... well, everything. Why is Marvin a robot, you might ask yourself. The reason is obvious. Living beings tend to want to hang on to little shreds of hope. They are incapable of the sort of honesty that oozes from Marvin's circuits. Yet isn't it a little, oh, I don't know, reassuring to just admit that everything sucks, it's never going to get any better, that you were born in obscurity and are going to die in debt? I find it tiring, the constant, it's always darkest before the dawn, every cloud has a silver lining crap that people will try to force down your throat in a futile attempt to make you feel better. It forces you to constantly strive to do better, which, let's face it, is mostly just a waste of time. Marvin = Truth.

Of course Eddie is the Yin to Marvin's Yang, a computer you just want to slap, always eager to please, always happy to do any task. Eddie is the lies we are fed by the media; you know that all people are successful, thin, healthy and well loved. They also have lots of sex when they drive the right car. Eddie = Lies.

These equations become obvious when we see that the crew of the *Heart of Gold* are often annoyed with Marvin—because aren't we always annoyed by the truth? But they openly dislike and at times distrust Eddie. Why? Because no one likes or trusts a liar, just ask your mother.

The improbability drive—this is a stroke of pure geniuses. I mean, things that shouldn't happen in a million billion years happen all the time. People choke to death on pudding. Normal parents give birth to truly stupid children, while idiot people have brilliant kids. Ugly—and broke-assed—men date beautiful women. Imagine the boon to society when we learn to harness the energy of improbability. Hell, we could light the entire northeastern seaboard for a hundred years just on the results of the 2000 presidential election and Anna Nicole Smith having a successful TV show.

Need still more proof that *Hitchhiker's* isn't fiction at all but an actual factual guide about our universe? It is now common knowledge that stress and nervous tension are the major source of several different diseases. We now know just how bad stress is for us, and if we occasionally forget it's a sure bet that some asshole will remind us. But *Hitchhiker's* was first copyrighted in 1979. Parents were still screaming at their children on sitcoms back then; no one knew stress was dangerous, we all thought it was funny. Yet Douglas Adams was so concerned with not causing us any unnecessary stress that he went ahead and told us that the planet in question was Magrathea, that the deadly missiles were only going to break some cups and bruise someone and that further, the bruising was inconsequential.

He knew!

Let us ponder for a moment the fate of the misfortunate whale. The Hebrew Bible clearly states in the book of Genesis that on the second day, God separated the water from the land, but it wasn't till the fifth day that God made creatures to inhabit the waters. And as has already been pointed out, there are five books in the holy trilogy. Five books; on the fifth day of creation, sea creatures were created. So we now clearly see that the entire whale story is not simply put there for our amusement, but has a deep and spiritual meaning.

The whale is scarcely come into being when he crashes to the surface of Magrathea—whose inhabitants had created the planet on which whales came into being—and dies. Read carefully, if you will, the words the whale thinks upon being zapped into being. "What's happening? Who am I? Why am I here? What's my purpose?" Then just as he starts putting things together, giving form to his thoughts, wondering if he can make friends—smack, it's all over.

The fate of the whale is also a metaphor for the fate of all whales if we continue to pollute the oceans as we have. There are layers upon layers. See how deep and mysterious are the ways of the sacred text?

Also according to the Bible, God created plants on the third day. Three being the number of books one normally associates with a trilogy. Petunias are a plant, and while the whale is pondering its existence and all its related aspects as he hurtles toward his cruel fate, all the petunias think is, "Oh no, not again."

Further, "Mr. Adams" goes on to write that if we knew why they thought that, we'd be a lot closer to figuring out the universe than we are.

So what does all this mean? Does *Hitchhiker's* parallel the Bible? Are plants smarter than sea mammals? Is three the same as five?

I'm not sure. Of course. Maybe. And only if you're dyslexic.

Earth is of course 42—the computer which was built according to calculations made by Deep Thought—not to be mistaken for Deep Throat, which gets one to stop thinking about the answer to the Ultimate Question, which isn't necessarily a bad thing—to answer Life, the Universe, and Everything. It is important to note now that three will go into 42 fourteen times, while five goes in eight times with a remainder of two. Now, there are nine planets in our solar system. Nine plus eight equals seventeen, and if you subtract the number of the remainder—which is two—you get fifteen. We have one sun, and if you subtract one from fifteen you get fourteen.

Scary, huh?

Now, you most probably think that Slartibartfast is just a silly name Douglas Adams made up. This simply isn't so, for if you break down the different groups of letters it is soon revealed to you that LART is fast Bart. No one knows who Bart is; however, LART is the anagram for Landing At Roughly Two, which is faster than Landing At Roughly One. This is obviously a message designed especially for Bart, and is a portent of things that will come to pass toward the end of days.

Of course Landing At Roughly Two (LART) might also be a location, and we should all be looking for the time when Fast Bart will land roughly at latitude two.

As with most sacred texts, the meaning is sometimes unclear and requires much study and meditation. Does not the first tome of the great text clearly state at the beginning of chapter twenty-three...and I quote, "It is an important and popular fact that things are not always what they seem."

At the time of the great On-Turning, when Lunkwill and Fook activate Deep Thought, they immediately have to deal with the problem that the perfection they set out to create is flawed. Far from being the answer to their Ultimate Question, it gives them yet another problem. They must create another computer, a truly superior computer, and none of them will have the answer till they are all dead for many millions of years. At which point, what does knowledge—even absolute knowledge—really matter at all?

Doesn't this in fact mirror the futility of parenthood? We have our first child, we expect they will be perfect and bring completion to our lives. Then we take them home and we begin to notice a few flaws. They crap their pants—that's not very bright—one eye seems to wonder around looking at...well, nothing that you can see. They mostly drool and spit up and keep you up all night, which does nothing to increase your hope that they will eventually be perfect.

As they grow you become increasingly, alarmingly, aware of the fact that they're really not that bright at all. So you have another, to see if they might come out better. Some people in fact just keep trying and trying. Of course, in the end you die and your bones are dust before they ever amount to anything, and if you ever do you won't know anything about it!

But I'm not bitter.

Let us now look at what happens when it looks as if Deep Thought is about to answer the Ultimate Question. Who should show up but the clergy. And what do they want? To shut down the program. What is the not-so-hidden meaning? That religious leaders don't want us to know the truth. Historically, religious institutions have been responsible for hindering the quest for knowledge at almost every turn.

A modern example of this is the insistence that the only sort of sex education we offer our children is abstinence. Religious leaders think it's wrong to tell teenagers about condoms. "That," they say, "encourages them to have sex."

This is, of course, completely wrong. *Hormones* encourage teenagers to have sex. Since many of us were born as a result of "abstinence only" sex education, it has been proven that it does not work. Yet they insist that it does. Why? Because, as the good book tells us, if we have the true answers, then religious leaders are flat out of their jobs.

In order to stay in power they must have "rigidly defined areas of doubt and uncertainty."

Which is why, of course, Douglas Adams was forced to publish *The Hitchhiker's Guide to the Galaxy* as a science fiction book instead of a religious text.

They don't want you to know the truth!

The Holy Trilogy brings enlightenment and comfort to those who begin to see its ultimate truth. What could be more comforting than to know that everyone in the universe is paranoid, believing that there is something going on that we know nothing about, something big and even sinister, and being told that this condition is perfectly normal?

"I'd rather be happy than right." That's Inspirational.

"Don't forget your towel." Wiser words have never been spoken.

The towel, that which does wipeth up what we spillith, be it milk or blood. The towel, which should go with us everywhere we travel.

The towel symbolizes our desire for knowledge, for does a towel not soak things up? And if you don't then rinse the towel out, does it not get stinky and moldy and then rot? So, too, must we soak up knowledge, then process it and spill it out, or our brains will get moldy and stinky and rotten.

The towel also symbolizes comfort, for it dries us when we're wet, and can be placed upon the bar stool when we're about to sit in the bar at the nudist colony our weird cousin Ernie talked us into going to on our vacation—and wasn't that the worst five hundred bucks you ever spent and is it really polite for people to point and laugh?

Anyway...

Heed well the words, "...careless talk costs lives." How can you doubt that these are divine words when the proof is all around you? Hell, every time a politician gives a speech people die.

I have barely scratched the surface. Did you know that there are pictures of towels on the walls of Egyptian tombs and temples in South America? Aborigines used to worship towels...Well, maybe worship is a little strong, but they did really, really like them.

Ford is the name of a car, which isn't perfect and oftentimes isn't even close. I suppose you think that has no significance at all.

In closing, I would like to quote Slartibartfast "...the chances of finding out what is really going on are so absurdly remote that the only thing to do is to say hang the sense of it and just keep yourself occupied."

How can you argue with wisdom like that?

Selina Rosen is the author of *Queen of Denial, Recycled,* the Chains trilogy, and the creator and editor of the *Bubbas of the Apocalypse* universe. Her short fiction has appeared in *Sword and Sorceress, Turn the Other Chick,* and the *Thieves' World* anthologies. She was told by...well, almost everyone that there was no market for the sort of weird, humorous sci-fi she was writing. When she first saw Douglas Adam's work, she knew the world was wrong.

Marie-Catherine Caillava

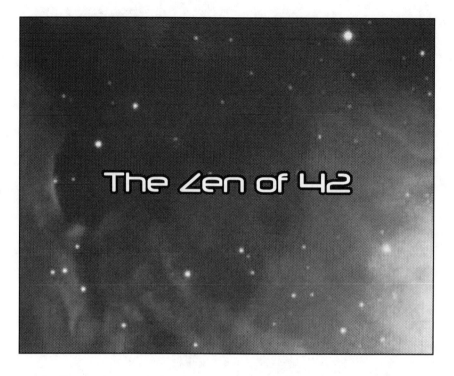

The Zen of 42

So far we've established that Douglas Adams was a computer scientist genius, an oracle of our times, the true inventor of Wikipedia and the Internet and a philosopher of humor. Turns out he's also a Zen master.

WAS DOUGLAS NOEL ADAMS a tall fellow from the U.K. who wrote comedy science fiction in the British nonsense style, or was he a Zen master who enlightened the life of many people through his Zen-for-all manual called The Hitchhiker's Guide to the Galaxy?

This question probably never occurred to most readers of H2G2. After all, DNA's masterpiece is both comedy and sci-fi, and at first sight it's not related to East Asian philosophy. Take another wonder of the British humor: *Monty Python's Flying Circus*—it's incredibly funny, disturbing, socially provocative, but has nothing to do with Zen. Or consider the root of all British sci-fi: *Doctor Who*—it's clever, thought-provoking, scary and bizarre, but still has nothing to do with mysticism or religion, even when it asks questions about the deep nature of man.

So, was Doug Adams a tall Brit Zen master or a tall Brit funny-sci-fi writer? To answer this question, we'll have to search our memories.

Breathe in slowly, look around you again to check and make sure no sales attendant in the bookshop has yet spotted you hidden behind the self-improvement shelf reading this, and try to concentrate. Try with all your might to remember what it felt like when you first read H2G2. Was it just a good laugh? Did you say: "Ah, my ribs hurt but I needed that. I haven't laughed so hard since my brother-in-law fell into the icebox!" Or was your reaction only: "Gee, what imagination Mr. Adams has. It's all much more convincing science fiction than *Star Trek*—a two-headed guy, a rock group so loud it can blast planets and small furry creatures that are real small furry creatures. That's just as good as Asimov's robots stories!" Or was your reaction more along the lines of: "Yes, Douglas Adams has a flamboyant imagination and is a brilliant humorist, but there is more than comedy or sf to The Hitchhiker's Guide. There is something in there that makes the word 'intelligence' float in my brain, something that makes me see things around me in a different way—and not just digital watches and the number forty-two, but life, the universe, everything and...hum, I think I'll read it again right now."

If you did react in that manner, like many readers did around our suburbia-type planet, then you have unknowingly answered "Yes" to the question "Was Douglas Adams a Zen master?" We have to face the fact that a man capable of imagining the Improbability Drive out of scratch has something you and I haven't got. Some might call it genius. Some, who generally don't wear digital watches because, to them, time is a double illusion and lunchtime triply so, would call it Enlightenment.

Adams never tried to hide the real nature of his opus. H2G2 is just posing as comedy and sci-fi. The author makes it very clear from the first page on. The scene he sets is actually, and most obviously, about mystical and philosophical concepts. Page one states that people on Earth can be defined by the fact that they are always unhappy and no one knows why or what to do about it. Adams goes on, a few pages later, with the Earth being destroyed in the most pitiful manner and for the most futile reason. Yes, in DNA's universe death is inevitable. Poor lovely planet, says Ford, walking away from the cavemen, it only has a few million years to live and that's it. Robots are depressive, cavemen are nice folks—something which would be good news, except for the fact that we are not their grandkids, as we descend from stupid, boring, petty bureaucrats who crash-landed on Earth with their rubber ducks and meeting agendas. Those poor idiots were themselves kicked off their planet because of their mediocrity. A good move from the government of that planet, one could think. But no, not in DNA's world: everybody died on Golgafrincham because the morons were not there to sanitize the phones anymore, and everybody died of phone poisoning—you can't get more human than that. Even mighty interstellar fleets get eaten by small dogs. As for characters, they are surprisingly not fun to be with: Arthur is as kind and boring as a cold cup of tea, Ford is persistently weird, Zaphod has two brains which he alternatively uses to be in love with himself and to deny disturbing facts, Trillian is so smart that she could not and should not be so disturbingly lovely, Fenchurch is so real and normal that she does not belong in such a zany world even when she flies, and machines are so much like people they are not worth mentioning.

Comedy is about escaping our boring daily lives, seeing the bright or ridiculously funny side of things. Pop science fiction ("pop" as in "first conceived for TV or radio") is basically about teams of incredibly smart and slim people visiting puzzling alien places and pondering the greatness of man and what a brilliant idea it was to create NASA in the first place.

Doug Adams never tried to fool anybody about the genre of his work.

H2G2 is a trilogy of five books, filled with brilliant plot ideas, jokes, witty dialogues and enough incredible mind-blowing ideas to feed Hollywood's industry for two centuries, and within all that, Adams makes it crystal clear: doomed and stupid, that's what we are, us and our universe. But does it mean that Adams' work is a depressive and hopeless one? No. But it definitely asks the big anguishing questions. Questions DNA himself states in simple unambiguous terms: it's all about life, the universe and everything. Questions so big no one and no computer has thought of them yet.

If H2G2 is about metaphysics, is there a God in its universe? A God person seems to be around in *The Hitchhiker's Guide*, but his credibility is zero. He apologizes in fire-like letters, but in a tone that reminds us of the public announcements in the ever-out-of-service-somewhere London Tube. If that God had spoken and not written, he would have had a female flight attendant's voice.

What about wise men? There is one character who fits the identikit of a wise old master. Actually, he talks and looks so much like Gandalf that we can't imagine anybody but Sir Ian McKellen for the part. But the old fellow is not wise; he is ridiculous, has a laughable name and can't handle basic threats or jokes.

No father image, no God, a universe we see die each time the dessert trolley passes by at Milliways, no future for our planet, no afterlife for our souls if we have any, and no interesting people. Just us, boring and blinded by our wee daily problems. Arthur wants some tea, Marvin wants to win, Zaphod looks for a mirror, Ford needs a fix (of what he doesn't seem to know himself), the old bearded man has a tantrum because he wants to make fjords around Africa. As for our planet—along with the great question to the great answer to everything—it vanishes because of a second-class road being constructed by a boring and petty (what, he is *that* too?) alien and his ugly ship of bored bureaucrats and bad cooks.

Perhaps DNA wanted to tell us that psychology is the answer to our despair. No, he does not. In his universe, shrinks are selfish, scheming and pretentious; they are "just this guy." In fact Adams tells us that everything, from rubber ducks to the universe itself, is "just this guy."

But what's with that Zen thing, then? (Try and say that sentence very fast, two hundred times.)

Zen tells us that we should give up our delusions. There are no beliefs, no trust, faith or admiration for anyone or anything, and therefore no delusion in Adams' work. We might detect here and there a bit of depression maybe, but DNA's universe is very much active, and not in a blues-induced paralysis. It's relentlessly searching for an answer...sorry, I meant for a question. A question, for we are so pitiful and laughable in the world of two-headed men and real small furry creatures that we, sentient beings, don't even look for answers. We already have answers. But we don't understand them, because we don't have the questions.

What do we have?

The number forty-two, and a towel.

And Nothingness. Lots of it.

The scene is all set without any ambiguity by Master Adams. Arthur could well have said the historical words barked at terrified passersby in Oxford during WWI by young Christmas Humphreys, the man who introduced Zen to the United Kingdom: "What is it all about?"

Interestingly, the Japanese word "Zen" very literally means "nothing," except of course in California, where it means "cool" or "good word to add to any title to make it sell, as in "Zen and the art of throwing your brother-in-law in the icebox just for fun."

Reading any serious book about Zen will have one immediate effect on you: it will help you realize how ignorant, boring and stupid you are. Just like H2G2 does. It's a small world, isn't it?

Zen is one way, among many others, of practicing Buddhism. It says that life is made of pain and dissatisfaction. Arthur, who is the alter ego of the reader, would totally agree with that statement, and with good reason. His point of view about life only differs from Marvin's in that he is still hoping and fighting when the android has given up the search. Zen goes on saying that pain can be replaced by Enlightenment, provided we realize that the ego is an illusion, that the part of us which says "what about *me*, what about *me*" is a delusion. If one were to name a person, either real or fictional, who is the ultimate embodiment of that tight-minded and blindly self-centered attitude, Zaphod would do perfectly.

Buddhas and Zen masters have repeatedly told us for 2,500 years that all things are in fact one, a theory also known in glasses-wearing circles as non-duality. You, I mean you, holding this book (if you are holding *this manuscript* it means you are my publisher—I bow down, but I still mean *you*) are a human being, but you are also the tree in the courtyard, the first Buddha, your neighbor and even your brother-in-law—which is why it would be very stupid of you to push him into the icebox for a laugh (throwing yourself in the fridge would be just as idiotic). The fun news is that everybody and everything else, including your dog and one of the atoms in that shelf over there, are all those things too. They are also you-I-mean-you, obviously.

The awareness of this non-duality appears in Douglas Adams' work most clearly in the epilogue to *Life, the Universe and Everything*. Arthur, thanks to the Bistromathic drive, realizes that all is one: mind and universe, perception and reality, time and space. The paragraph I'm refer-ring to could be a direct quote from any Zen book. The fact that this concept is presented to us by Adams as the thoughts of a fictional char-acter is irrelevant: who thought them, who invented both them and the character thinking them? Adams, of course.

To Buddhists, there is no God, at least not in the sense of a God person with a defined personality, will and moods. (Buddha is no God; the Very Wise died at the age of eighty of food poisoning—you can't be more human than that.)

The man at the figurative center of the universe in H2G2 answers the question "Do you rule the universe?" by the very Zen-riddle-like phrase: "I try not to." Master Daruma, founder of Zen, was once asked by the mighty Emperor of China, "What is Zen?" He answered: "Noth-ing special." The Emperor insisted: "But who are you?" Daruma simply retorted: "I haven't got the faintest idea!" and left.

The tone is strikingly similar: disturbingly anticlimatic, thought-pro-voking and simply funny. Daruma's words and what Mr. I-Try-Not-To says could be interchanged and still be in character.

Another word that has been misused a lot, again in California, is "Karma." Karma just means action. If you let a bowl of petunias fall from a planetary orbit, it will crash on the ground. If you do something detrimental to anyone, to anything or to yourself, the law of cause and effect will have you face the consequences—it's not a punishment, just a law of nature. The eternal tug-of-war between Arthur and all of his vic-tims' reincarnations (reincarnation, another Buddhist concept), wheth-er animal or vegetal, follows that very law: bad Karma, even if created accidentally by Arthur, causes bad Karma—here, hatred and desires of revenge in his victim. Result: tragedy for everybody, poor petunias, poor bat and most of all poor Arthur.

One thing specific to Buddhism is that there is no doctrine, no "you must believe in *this* or you're not a Buddhist." There is not even a con-version ceremony (this might be why so many people turn toward Buddhism—that spares them being offered two hundred gold fountain pens). That is also why there is no official opinion of Buddhism about anything, no Pope, no fighting among factions about the right place for a comma in the scriptures. Buddha himself wrote that his teachings were just a pointer, but not the goal, and should be left behind when becoming useless, just like a raft should be abandoned once the shore has been reached.

The actual main character of H2G2, referred to as "the Book" in the original radio show, has a lot of high pretensions. It claims at length to be the ultimate guide to the universe, and even to be able to help you keep your cool. The words "Don't Panic," written on the cover, helped it become so popular throughout the Galaxy. But when it comes to actually helping you, this Book is incredibly useless. It describes Earth as harmless or mostly so—in either case a lie; when DNA wrote the original show, during the late seventies, the vicinity of our planet was not exactly harmless. The Book also tells you, for example, that to get help or a drink from a Vogon the solution is "forget it." Not very helpful. Even Ford, one of the professional researchers of the volume, gets stranded, lost in time, baffled and out of booze, just like a greenhorn in the old West. So much for the big mighty text that, we eventually learn, has been mostly copied from the back of a breakfast cereal box.

What Adams is telling us here is that maps are useless when it comes to facing the terrain, that the teachings are empty and full of lies and that "useful" books are all shams. We are on our own to face whatever horror looms (and it does loom a lot in the H2G2 universe!). The words "Don't Panic" sound as empty as the jolly song "Look upon the bright side of life," whistled merrily by the crucified innocents in the very controversial *Monty Python's Life of Brian*. Words, words, words. They can't help at all. And Adams often employs the humoristic device of using big impressive words by the dozen, only to deflate the effect they were beginning to create in our mind, thereby making us see them in a plain and grotesque way. The scene of the Great On-Turning of Deep Thought in the first volume, with its over-the-top, grandiose and increasingly pompous vocabulary, ends with "tricky." Almost any paragraph about the Book is written in this mode.

The Zen school tells us that Enlightenment, also known as *satori*, simply means a sudden realization. Being enlightened means being in the now (our body always is, but our mind almost never) and seeing the universe, including ourselves and things we firmly believe in, just as they actually are.

The Total Perspective Vortex is probably the most brilliant Zen teaching tool ever invented since the day the Very Wise sat under the Bodhi tree and was himself enlightened. It's a good thing that that Vortex is only a fictional one. For if it did exist, it would actually drive the user insane, just like it does in *The Hitchhiker's Guide*. This invention alone marks Adams as a genius, and a Zen one at that.

The concept behind the TPV is about seeing what we actually are in the universe, thanks to a blinding snapshot of the said universe taken by a machine that uses a piece of cake as the universe template (since the cake is part of the universe, it contains it all. Another perfect and clear expression of the central idea in Zen that all is one; the cake is the universe and the universe is the cake). As for us, you and me, poor boring and petty humans, full of certitudes about who is the most intelligent race of creatures on Earth, or what Earth is exactly, we would indeed go mad if we realized what we and our world as we see it really are. Adams was stating a fact about his brainchild machine.

Describing the Total Perspective Vortex is describing Zen, precisely, exactly and almost fully. It also tells us why traditional Zen training, as dispensed in monasteries, is very careful and progressive. But most people, especially in Occident, don't have the patience or tenacity to study such a discipline so slowly. A perfect avatar of us is President Zaphod. The inventor of the Gargle Blaster is indeed magnificently hopeless. Any character in the book, other than he, upon seeing that the machine's answer is "You are the center of the universe," would have said: "Wait a minute, this is fishy!" But Zaphod does not need his special glasses to be in denial about dangers. Some of us, indeed many of us, do the same every day—take the good news without thinking and deny the bad news, even if it means facing the consequences later. Zen has been created to help us, those who want to be helped; that is, not Zaphod, obviously.

We laugh, or giggle, or constantly smile while reading or listening to H2G2. Zen and humor are old partners. Zen masters have systematically and continuously used nonsense and humor for almost 2,500 years now. So much for the British inventing nonsense (if you have never heard a Zen master laugh, you don't know what freedom sounds like).

Zen uses riddles, or jokes that are either nonsensical and/or unsolvable. In Japanese they are called *koans*. The most famous one in Occident is probably: "What is the sound of one hand clapping?" DNA's humor is in perfect tune with *koans*. It does not just make us smile. The following quote (the intro pages to *Mostly Harmless*, a book we cannot exactly describe as optimistic) can hardly be labeled as just fun or just silly or even simply entertaining, though these *are* funny and clever lines too. There is much deepness of thought in this series of deceptively obvious statements. I quote Master Adams:

> Anything that happens, happens.
> Anything that, in happening, causes something else to happen, causes something else to happen.

Anything that, in happening, causes itself to happen again, happens again.
It does not necessarily do it in that order, though.

This type of nonsensical rhetoric, that says a lot but implies even
more, is at the heart of Zen training. To quote but one great *koan* writer,
Master Dogen, one of the greatest in the history of Zen:

> To learn the Buddha's way is to learn one's self
> To learn one's self is to forget one's self
> To forget one's self is to be confirmed by all teachings.

Same mystic ideas, same style of writing and identical type of wit.
Adams' intro to another of the H2G2 books states that the universe will
be replaced by something more complex if anybody figures out what it's
actually like. This, again, is in the same vein as Zen statements such as,
"The moment you talk about Zen, Zen escapes away from you."
Zen tells us that we fill our lives with useless chatter and toys to avoid
facing reality. Ford Prefect developed the theory that humans must talk
all the time, saying useless things like, "You have a British accent, Mr.
Adams," or, "It's a bit chilly in this bookshop," else their brains will start
working and they'll go nuts. Once again Zen and Douglas Noel Adams
say the same things, using the same tools.
Zen masters also insist that logic is just as useless as words. Oolon
Colluphid wrapped it up for God, as Doug Adams played with logic to
show that, if I may formulate it as a mathematical equation to make
things simpler:

> God *minus* Faith *plus* Babel fish, *to the power of* man's insufferable
> know-it-all logic, *equals* black is white, *which creates a vector of*
> "Hey, mind that bus, what bus?—oops, too late!" at next zebra
> crossing.

Zen leads us to laugh at ourselves. Adams did too—laugh at himself
and his readers: "...an old solitary man who claimed repeatedly that
nothing was true, though he was discovered later to be lying" is one of
my favorite *tee-hee* jokes in the whole series. (It's not a *koan*, as it doesn't
call for an answer.)
I hear some reader suggest, "What about vegetarianism? Most Buddhists are; that's a Zen thing if ever." It is, and Adams brilliantly ad-

vocated it with a mind-bogglingly inescapable trap for the reader. I'm talking, of course, about the scene at Milliways, when the fact that the cow wants to be eaten disgusts Arthur to the verge of sickness, just before he realizes, along with the horrified reader, that eating a cow that does *not* want to be eaten (something he's done all his life) is even more horrible. The joke about the cow preparing to kill itself in a "humane" way is a direct kick in the chin to those who, in the late seventies, advocated that eating living creatures was all right as long as they did not suffer when slaughtered.

What part of Zen could remain that has not been illustrated most brilliantly by Master Adams in his masterpiece? Intelligence and power of analysis? It's there, for example, in the three phases of civilization being defined as how we eat, why we eat, where we eat. A serious sociological-historical thesis could be written by developing those lines alone. They contain enough thought and truth to be turned into a 200-page discourse. DNA only wrote a few sentences about it, not because he could not make it grow more, but because he had 3,000 other ideas pushing this one out and away.

Zen advocates keeping a "beginner's mind," saying that to a beginner all options are open, but a person with training has preconceived ideas that do close certain doors to him or her. This can be found in Fenchurch and Arthur's art of flying. The concept that to fly, you just have to forget to fall is invented, developed and explained by Adams in the most convincing way. While you read it, it makes perfect sense, even if it's, indeed, very, very funny. The innocence, the "beginner's mind," is the secret to flight.

The case of "Adams the great Zen master" versus "Adams, just this witty sci-fi-writing guy" seems to be very sound. Clues and proofs are aplenty; not one link has been left out. Could DNA actually have been a Zen master without *even* knowing it? Witness, please! Let's just ask him.

Ford Prefect, his brainchild, a part of himself, gives us the answer: "In an infinite universe, anything can happen, even survival."

Zen masters have often said that Zen is about everyday life, about nothing *special*, and that those who talked a lot about it were still searching for it—fools who did not even realize it was in them all along. If one is to accept such a concept, would it not be possible for a man to be a master without knowing it? The Southern Patriarch, a great master if ever, was illiterate and only heard one sentence of a Buddhist text when he understood life, the universe and everything. Was he just a cook or a master? The abbot who chose him as his successor thought that he was a master.

If this is true, then The Hitchhiker's Guide to the Galaxy is indeed a Zen manual that aims at awaking the reader by making him face some realities that are not easy to accept. Humor, science fiction—what better tools to lure the reader, to make him get so involved in the plot and the puns that he won't even notice before it's too late that...say, come to think of it, could the Earth and myself and the universe be something else than what I thought?

Clever Master Adams, who did so much, and so discreetly, for the Enlightenment of...oh, all right, let's be realistic: of course, *obviously*, Adams never realized how much Zen there was in his books, and never actually meant to put it there. He did not sit at his typewriter thinking: "Right, I'll make it a radio show, and when nobody suspects anything, I'll make a series of books, and people will see Zen at work and become wiser; meanwhile I'll try not to notice that I'm a master myself."

All great and good men have intuitions pointing toward the same concepts. Emperor Marcus Aurelius, King Solomon, Pharaoh Akhenaton and many others. Nobody would say these men knew about Zen. Yet they all pointed in the same direction: you and the others are one, life is pain, what happens is a consequence of what has happened, the world is not what it seems. Many less famous wise men have had the same intuition of what has been developed fully into Zen. Let's call it the "Wise Fellows" club.

Douglas Adams, like many other laymen plagued with the disease called genius, was a member of that so-select club. He had a very high IQ, loads of culture, plus some obvious interests in the "big questions." He was born in a time and place where philosophies from the East were beginning to merge with those of the West.

A study of Douglas Adams' complete work shows that he was an atheist (as is clear in his interviews); a man who loved technology as long as it helped people (re: his writings about Apple computers—you can find all these at www.douglasadams.com); a strong advocate of animal rights (some of his articles contain ideas that are cheered at by the most hard-line vegans); an ecologist with no illusions about mankind (read *Last Chance to See*, a book about all the wonders of nature that are about to disappear courtesy of Man's Stupidity and Greed ™). He believed in sharing knowledge with all, as his work on the Internet showed.

A quick look at his other major works, for example the Dirk Gently books and *Starship Titanic*, confirm that there was, so to speak, Zen in his blood.

Dirk Gently, Adams' Holistic Detective, had a very special way of working: he considered that everything leads to everything else in this one-is-all universe. So if he was investigating a murder in London, he'd go buy an ice cream in Japan to find a lead, and it worked.

The Zen flavor, the Zen way of thinking that we find on every page of H2G2, was no accident at all. Douglas Adams had it all in him. He was of the "Wise Fellows" club.

This wisdom and compassion might also explain the love his friends and family had for him. I was in Rome the day he died. I remember how I scanned the newsgroup at www.douglasadams.com to get information, hoping to read: "Sorry, it's a joke, Doug is OK." I ended up talking to some Italian fans, all in shock, like me. We met on Piazza Navona, a towel on our shoulder to recognize each other. Later that night, as we were still mentally running in circles, trying to deny it all, I got a call from a friend in Montreal. Over there, too, they were trying to talk it away, or for some, drink it away. We were all staggered when we realized how many of "us" there were worldwide, how many people considered they owed a lot to Douglas Adams.

I doubt that the death of any other modern writer—even those who passed away untimely—caused such worldwide emotion when they died.

Douglas Adams. A nonviolent ape descendant, full of love for life in all its forms, full of anguish and despair about mankind's stupidity, a man with intuitions that labeled him clearly a genius and not "just" a comedy sci-fi writer, even if he was that too. A tall Brit fellow with the intelligence to question all things and still laugh at himself and his world.

Was Doug a Zen master?

Does it really matter?

Zen is there, under each stone of Magrathea, in the brain wave patterns of Arthur. Some of us, who have felt pleasantly disturbed by the philosophy underlying Arthur's predicaments, will look in other books, books with the word "Zen" in the title. But, in the end, it all will get to the same conclusion: there is a big question about life, the universe and everything.

Forty-two is the answer to that question.

But what is or is not the question?

Oh, what a lovely *koan*. Thanks again, Master Adams, or thanks again, Doug. It's the same thing anyway, if all things are one, as the Bistromathic drive has taught us.

Marie-Catherine Caillava lives in London. She's a ghostwriter, translator and radio critic specializing in SF. She is currently still trying to recover from translating *Starship Titanic* into French. Her hobbies are Zen calligraphy, Kyudo (traditional archery), traveling to Japan and getting her dog to stop barking at the TV set when she watches cartoons. But not necessarily in that order, though.

Mark W. Tiedemann

Loop-Surface Security: The Image of the Towel in a Vagabond Universe— A Semiotic (Semi-Odd) Excursion

According to postmodernism, there is no absolute truth, no absolute reality. You don't exist and neither do I. In fact, these words don't exist and I'm not writing them. There are no deadlines. I could go home right now and take a nap, except that there is no home, and no such thing as a nap. Or something like that. It's a bit complex, but I do believe that even postmodernists could agree on one fundamental reality: the importance of the towel.

DOUGLAS ADAMS' REPEATED INABILITY to find his towel during a stay with friends led to an assumption of a standard of competence not commonly accepted by most humans on Earth. In milieus concerned with academic skill, physical prowess, cleverness, ruthlessness and appearance as standards of competence, it is often the ordinary, the mundane and the overlooked daily materials of life that may be the true tests of our ability to cope. Only by their absence do such things rise to general notice.

How does one convey the importance of such an object? First, it requires that we recognize something fundamental about the object. Then we must understand how its meaning, its importance, shifts with a change in context. Where we find a particular sign/object, and in relation to what other objects, in the landscape in which it resides, determines its meaning. Altering any one of these factors also alters the object's meaning.

Adams demonstrated a superb grasp of these fluid concepts by constructing an elaborate fictive context, the entire purpose of which is to spotlight the importance of the object under examination. Perhaps, he must have reasoned, by displacing humans to an environment off Earth, the true relevance of the object—the towel (at least, the knowledge of where one's is)—would become obvious.

After all, the towel is what the Hitchhiker's Guide to the Galaxy series is all about.

(Many arguments have been put forward to suggest that it is about other things—interstellar travel, dictionaries, travel guides, Kensington parties, irony, or even the Ultimate Question—but the only aspect of the work that is repeatedly shown to retain its semiotic force is the towel.)

Ford Prefect's cautionary imperative to Arthur Dent—that if one is to survive, one must know where one's towel is—reflects this assumption. Of all the things that might have occurred to Arthur during the chaos (personal and otherwise) in the period surrounding Earth's destruction, hanging on to a towel would probably not be one of them, even though he made a cursory bow to custom by donning a bathrobe before confronting the work crew determined to demolish his house.

The circumstances of that reflexive nod to public modesty shows an underlying pattern determining the way symbols are read in human society—at least as understood in that area at that time. Given the imminence of the situation—bulldozer, crew, public works decree to demolish a private home—everyone readily accepted Dent's hasty emergence from that same house in pajamas and bathrobe. Indeed, had he taken a few minutes to change into standard trousers, a shirt and shoes, some might have questioned the authenticity of emotion that drove his subsequent actions: confrontation, mock-sacrificial lying upon the ground to impede an admittedly unimpedable force, stubborn refusal to accommodate what some might see as The Inevitable. Changing clothes would signify a degree of calm, perhaps even a lack of concern, which would lead to questions of motive. Perhaps the house meant less to Dent than he avowed. Dressing properly might lead one to believe Dent had a sense of the potential celebrity inherent in the situation—lie there long enough, other people would learn of the stand-off, a news crew would show up; he would, for however brief a time, achieve notoriety, perhaps gain a modicum of authority. The potential, if well managed, would be enormous, leading to a career in politics, or possibly even the entertainment industry. If such were Dent's intention, dressing well would make sense. Indeed, some care might be required to select the right attire so as to make the greatest impact. Timing, in such a situation, would be key. If he took too long, the bulldozer might be through the front door before he could make his appearance to block it. Too hasty a choice, he would get his five minutes on the evening news and that would be the end of it.

Instead, there was no forethought. He did not prepare. He grabbed a bathrobe out of reflex and bolted from his house, disregarding the potential public impact of his appearance. This action, and his (automatic) choice of dress, served to underline the sincerity of his impulse, and in fact was perfectly understood and ultimately overlooked by everyone immediately involved.

But had he brought a towel with him, the reaction would have been very different.

Imagine you are on a demolition crew. You meet your coworkers, share coffee and donuts, draw your work orders for the day and proceed to the work site. As you, or one of your coworkers, directs the bulldozer toward the house designated for destruction, a man runs from the front door, clad in pajamas and bathrobe and carrying, tucked under one arm, a full-sized terrycloth bath towel.

The towel immediately alters your appreciation of this man. At once, you have to ask, "Is that a towel?" and then ask, "Why?" Both questions open the field to multiple interpretations of object and motive, neither of which can now be determined with any of the customary precision to which you have become accustomed in long years of knocking down houses. The towel, in brief, becomes more than an article of hygiene—which adds an important element to the context, given the man's intention of lying in the mud to block your bulldozer—but is now a destabilizing signifier. It renders the situation fluid because it puts you on your guard. Can you trust a man lying in the mud in his bathrobe and carrying a towel? If you challenge him, what will he do? The presence of the towel forces you to reconsider all your stock responses to unsettled homeowners who in the past have attempted to prevent you from doing your job. The towel is as effective in making you hesitate as a bullhorn, a billboard or a legal brief.

In fact, it is the absence of the towel that renders the scenario mundane.

It is the nature of symbols that they facilitate the construction of meaning both by their presence and their absence. Given the larger context and the ensuing series of events, the absence of the towel also becomes a potent symbol. It signifies Arthur Dent's failure.

(It is certainly legitimate to ask what would have changed if Dent had brought a towel to the confrontation. By extension, the inclusion of a towel in other confrontations could arguably have changed any number of documented outcomes. Imagine the shifts in outcome had Hamilton and Burr brought towels to their duel instead of pistols. Or if Congressman Preston Brooks had brought a towel instead of a cane to his confrontation with Senator Charles Sumner. Or if Nixon's famous Checkers speech had included an aside on Pat Nixon's new towels instead of a cloth coat—good Republican towels. To be sure, the towel has, in some contexts, become linked to surrender, vis a vis "throwing in the towel"—but that only applies when the towel is released. Hanging on to it by definition alters interpretation. Suppose, for example, Wittgenstein had been playing with a towel during Popper's presentation instead of a fireplace poker: the entire history of twentieth century philosophy might have taken a turn for the antic. "Give me an example of a moral rule!" "Not to threaten visiting lecturers with a towel." The consequences for both men's reputations are inestimable. After all, had Wittgenstein thrown a towel aside as he did the poker, the dispute between these two philosophers would have been settled with Wittgenstein conceding.)

Most humans leave their towels at home. The impact of this tradition-based negligence is inestimable. After all, in Adams' scenario, the entire planet is destroyed following a centuries-long tendency to ignore this most stable of symbols.

It is that very stability which draws our attention to the towel as the primary focus of the Hitchhiker's Guide to the Galaxy.

Yet it is a strange stability since, at base, it is the towel's similarity (as model) to the basic quantum structure of the universe that grounds its ultimate utility—a structure that begins and ends with indeterminacy.

We shall return to this in a moment.

Contemporary Western culture relies heavily on the towel, yet remarks upon it only occasionally. Bath towels, dish towels, hand towels, shop towels, beach towels, paper towels—all these forms serve one purpose: wiping up wet things. Drying. To be sure, this is a fundamental requirement in our society. We live in a particularly wet culture. Yet the inclusion of the towel in our daily activities rarely rises to a level of awareness that would indicate the degree of self-confidence or competence implicit in Ford Prefect's assertion that, "It's a rough universe out there…if you're going to survive, you've really got to know where your towel is."

In older traditions, the towel can be seen as a ritual element, dating back to the first Masses, and later as iconic emblems during weddings, births, deaths, house raisings and other indicators of alterations in social status. In some cultures, the towel is an heirloom requiring care in its passage from one generation to the next.

Such ritual signification—transforming an otherwise utilitarian object into, essentially, a metaphor—establishes a fundamental iconic use which transcends the mundane ones to which it is routinely put. It also establishes a strong link between object and user outside any linguistic limits set by expected forms. The utility of the object itself becomes multivarious, even under its common nomenclature. Consequently, knowing where one's towel is opens the field of possible interpretations to the near infinite, depending on context.

And this brings us, as previously suggested, to the towel's connection to the fundamental substructure of the universe.

Signs and symbols act linguistically as substitutes for actual objects—for, as it were, Reality. When using a sign, we make the fundamental assumption that there is in fact something it describes. The appropriation of a presumably stable sign to describe more than the presumptive primary object to which it refers (i.e., a towel as sign not for a roughly square or rectangular piece of terrycloth but for drying/hygiene/matching bathroom decor) stretches the possible uses of the sign through simile and metaphor. But even so, it is presumed, now that Derrida is dead, that something real is being described, that the sign is substituting for a presumptive object.

What, then, does a towel stand in for which would make knowing where it is the ultimate distinction of competence, indeed security, in this "rough universe"?

Knowing where an object is, according to quantum mechanics, is a most difficult task. Indeterminacy dominates any attempt to ascertain location and, consequently, relative motion. The problem is one of scale, since at the level of our senses everything seems perfectly fine. We know where the coffee cup from which we were drinking a few minutes ago is because we left it there. We can go directly to it, pick it up, carry it to the urn and refill it. It is in our hand at that point, we have a firm grasp on it and it isn't going anywhere we don't want it to go. Likewise the car (unless it's been stolen, which is often a consequence of current location, or because we've left it in an unfamiliar car park, ambled off to a bar and returned to find we can't remember where we left it), the refrigerator, our wallet (hopefully), and the book we were just reading. These objects do not arbitrarily shift position in space (though occasionally it seems they do) and, in a statistical sense, can be reliably found at precise spatial coordinates.

This holds true even for objects we presume to be in a given location without actually being able to see them. We know Washington, D.C., is where it is, even if most of us never go there, and that if we drive from the Midwest east on Interstate 70, then north on 79, Pittsburgh will be there.

Going further up in scale, we can make reasonable assumptions about the locations and velocities of comets, asteroids, planets and other stars. We can make a relatively safe assumption that by going *that* way long enough we will reach the star we call Betelgeuse. (Depending upon the accuracy of our initial assumptions, we may end up somewhere in the vicinity, but Betelgeuse will be where it is nonetheless.)

The trouble, however, reveals itself when we go in the opposite direction on the cosmic scale. The smaller the slice of reality we try to look at, the less reliable our ability to pin something down becomes. Quantum indeterminacy is the rule at the particle level of matter.

(Actually, an argument can be made—and will be here—that such indeterminacy is the rule at all levels, but demonstrable only through statistical analysis and by the behavior of a certain class of object, such as pencils, pens, guitar picks, car keys, winning lottery tickets and certain phone numbers, none of which can be reliably tracked over time.)

Physicist John Wheeler coined the term "Quantum Foam" to describe the roiling surface of the subatomic strata at its smallest dimension. The tendrils, coils and parabolic spasms give the universe a looped structure, bounding back and forth through time and infinitesimal distances. It is perhaps no coincidence that the fundamental structure of matter resembles foam. Foam is an excellent description of the subsequent indeterminacy inherent in the universe, and leads us to our best model for understanding the treacherous nature of reality as it rubs up against our perceptions.

Our ability to navigate in the universe, to reliably ascertain the position of a given object, to have a solid grasp of where we are, is like hanging on to a bar of wet soap. There is indeed a solid object, more or less in our grasp, but the nature of friction and foam render our hold tenuous at best. The bar can unpredictably and easily squirt from out hands, and our ability to retrieve it depends more on probability than any skill we may bring to bear.

Furthermore, by transference, the foam compromises our stability on particular surfaces. In order to reliably maintain balance and control, foam-slicked surfaces require contact with a loop-structured surface—carpet, or terrycloth.

Here some care is required not to make the erroneous assumption that it is *our* balance that is regained. Contact with the loop-structured surface says nothing about our stability and everything about the stability of the quantum model. Stepping from intractable tile to confidence-inspiring carpet does not mean that we now can make reliable statements about where we are or what we are doing. Rather, it demonstrates that the universe alone can make such reliable statements about itself.

Foam meets loop structure, and indeterminacy is resolved by mutual compatibility.

But we are discussing signs and symbols, not physics. Representational matrices (assemblies of words designed to more or less describe something) stand in for reality as linguistic devices, as conveniences of language. We presume the signs we choose and assign say something real about the objects to which they refer. To that end, descriptive similarities are valuable. And in that light, Adams' choice of the towel is infinitely viable in the context of stability.

Consider: the loop structure of towels mimics the fundamental substructure of the universe. Indeed, it is a stabilizing structure on its own, by its function of absorbing destabilizing moisture and foam.

The image of the towel becomes by extension a primary symbol of stability, particularly when the range of possible locations is increased vis-a-vis interstellar travel. The potential of universal application of the symbol suggests that the quantum model holds across cultures, regardless of divergent mythic traditions or cultural inconsistencies. The concept of indeterminacy would seem to be a commonly held belief. The towel, then, or its linguistic/semiotic equivalent, would be unconditionally understood.

The potency of the symbolism can be seen if one views the act of folding up a towel and tucking it in one's rucksack or under one's arm as the ritual equivalent of grabbing hold of a piece of the fundamental substructure of reality and claiming "This is mine and I know where it is!"

In conclusion, knowing where one's towel is becomes the sign equivalent of knowing where one's self is. While this linguistic assertion may lead to certain existentialist dilemmas (especially among the towelless or chronically insecure), it is the utility of the sign that matters here. The deployment of the sign—by, in fact, knowing where one's towel is—powerfully asserts the basic competence and, by extension, self-confidence of the user. Hence, through appropriation of a model of indeterminacy we can, in fact, banish indeterminacy, and lay claim to certitude, albeit a profoundly ironic one.

It is, indeed, about the towel.

Mark W. Tiedemann's love for science fiction began with an early viewing of *Forbidden Planet* and has continued unabated to the present day. His presumption that he could write was encouraged by his life companion, Donna, and he set out to publish. After attending Clarion in 1988, he began selling short fiction regularly. He has had stories in *Asimov's, F & SF, SF Age, Universe* and all three of the *Bending the Landscape* anthologies. Novels began appearing in 2001 with *Mirage*, the first in a new series of Asimov's robot stories. *Compass Reach*, volume one of the Secantis Sequence, was nominated for the Philip K. Dick Award in 2002. Aside from writing, he is an avid photographer (having made a living at it for close to thirty years) and sometime musician. *Remains* is his tenth book.

Jacqueline Carey

Yes, I Got It

Best-selling author Jacqueline Carey ponders the "subtle-ties" of British humor, her time as a bookstore clerk in London and getting it.

DURING THE PERIOD OF POST-COLLEGIATE AIMLESS-NESS which afflicts many young people possessed of a brand-new undergraduate degree with no immediate, practical real world value and no idea what to do with their lives, I spent six months participating in a work exchange program, working in a bookstore in London. It was a great experience which I highly recommend... but that's not the point.

The store where I worked wasn't one of those charming, idiosyncratic, Charing Cross Road types, evoking dusty tomes, hidden gems and tales of long-lost love. It was a branch of a local chain of bookstores, located in the City, the heart of the banking district. Picture the area where the father in *Mary Poppins* worked, if that helps. Very gray, lots of tall buildings. As a result, we didn't get many tourists there, just businessfolk on their lunch breaks. And conversely, our customers expected it to be a Yank-free zone.

One quiet afternoon, I was working the cash register at the rear of the store. A businesswoman in professional attire purchased a copy of *The Hitchhiker's Guide to the Galaxy*. The minute I opened my mouth, I was busted. "You're an American!" she said in a disapproving tone. I acknowledged that I was. She asked if I'd read the book, and I said that I had. The customer gave me a long, dubious look, then said, "Well, did you *get* it? Because the humor's quite British, you know. Subtle. Nothing like *yours*."

I assured her that yes, I'd gotten it, thinking to myself, "It ain't *that* subtle, lady!" At the time, our best-selling humorous book was a volume by British comedian Adrian Edmondson titled *How to Be a Complete Bastard*. As I recall, it had a lot of fart jokes, and it didn't leave me impressed with the overall caliber of British humor. However, rereading *The Hitchhiker's Guide* many years later, the exchange sticks in my mind. I stand by my opinion: although it doesn't rely on fart jokes, it's *not* that subtle. But the woman was right, too. There is a distinctly British flavor to the humor. Fortunately for the rest of us, it happens to travel well.

So what, exactly, makes it so British? And so funny?

For me, it has to do with a keen sense of the absurd, which often manifests in juxtaposing the outrageous and the mundane. Everything in Douglas Adams' universe, no matter how preposterous, has roots in the familiar. He has a knack for extrapolating the silliest aspects of the human experience and blowing them up into galactic proportions. Consider the towel—a largish bath towel from Marks and Spencer, in Ford Prefect's case. What item could be more homely? And yet this, *The Hitchhiker's Guide* tells us, is "about the most massively useful thing an interstellar hitchhiker can have." A series of suggested usages follows: a warm wrap, a beach blanket, a turban, a sail, a weapon of hand-to-hand combat.

And it's funny, damned funny, because we've all done it. We can relate. We may not shop at Marks and Spencer, but we've run around the beach with towels tied around our necks, pretending to be superheroes. We've wound them into turbans. We've spun them into damp, terry-cloth bullwhips and snapped them at our siblings' butts. It's just that we weren't bounding across the cold moons of Jaglan Beta or trudging across the desert world of Kakrafoon when we did. In fact, we were probably kids.

But we can picture it. And Adams makes it seem so . . . sensible. Anyone who's ever bummed around part of the world relying on a *Let's Go* or *Lonely Planet* guide resonates to the common-sense tenor of his advice. In a part of our minds, we nod and think to ourselves, "Yes, that's a very good point, that *would* be useful!" Until a sense of perspective reasserts itself, and we realize, no, that's just plain silly.

This brand of absurdity crops up over and over again. The green, bug-eyed monsters from outer space are irascible bureaucrats with a propensity for writing awful poetry. An extra arm? A handy thing to have. And when the *Heart of Gold* spaceship with the Improbability Drive reconfigures its interior . . . well, why shouldn't it put in some nice potted plants, a decorative staircase and a fish pond? It makes things ever so much more pleasant.

Samuel Taylor Coleridge wrote that imagination "reveals itself in the balance or reconciliation of opposite or discordant qualities: of sameness, with difference; of the general, with the concrete . . . the sense of novelty and freshness, with old and familiar objects."[1] I like to think that the old opium addict would be impressed by the extremes to which Adams takes this precept. I also like to think that my old college professors, the ones who mourned the loss of a promising young English major to the fickle siren song of commercial fiction, would be impressed that I not only retained the memory of that quote, but the *Theory of Literature* textbook in which to locate it. I am not, however, unduly optimistic.

---

[1] Samuel Taylor Coleridge, "Biographia Literaria," *Criticism: The Major Texts*, W.J. Bate, ed. (Harcourt Brace Jovanovich, 1970), p. 379

Adams does take it to extremes, constantly pushing the limits of absurdity. A pair of missiles turning into a sperm whale and a bowl of petunias several miles above an alien planet? Okay, it's amusing, and the Improbability Drive grants it a certain internal logic, without which the premise falls apart. But Adams isn't content to rest there. He gives us a thorough catalogue of the whale's thoughts throughout its brief, exuberant existence; and then, there's the bowl of petunias, which thinks to itself, "Oh no, not again."

A good novel often gives the reader the sense that it contains any number of stories, all of which the author could have told had he or she chosen to pursue them. Secondary characters enter in a trailing cloud of implicit backstory; they depart into the mists of untold further adventure. This is true of many novels, but in no other novel is it true of a bowl of petunias.

There's a wonderful economy to Adams' usage of language. In this, too, he revels in the absurd. Petunias. Why petunias? It's a precisely chosen flower, at once commonplace and utterly unexpected. It tickles the mysterious lobe of the brain where truly quirky humor abides. We have to laugh. Why is a bowl of petunias funnier than, say, a bowl of chrysanthemums? I don't know; but it is, unmistakably. Especially a sentient bowl of petunias.

The quintessential example, of course, is "forty-two," the answer to the Ultimate Question of Life, the Universe and Everything. One supposes it could have been almost anything, since the point of the answer is that it's the question that's ineffable. The beauty of "forty-two" lies not in its innate humor, but in that it goads the reader to periodically pause and think of hypothetical questions. Until, once again, we realize we're just being silly.

Throughout the book, there are countless other examples of Adams' skill in choosing his words with a poet's precision. One of my favorites lies in the description of Mr. L. Prosser, the petty bureaucrat and unwitting many-times-removed descendent of Ghengis Khan, whose ancestry manifests itself solely in a "pronounced stoutness about the tum and a predilection for little fur hats."

So simple…and so funny! And too, so very British. There's no affectionate American term for the midsection that would contrast quite as absurdly with the evocation of the great Mongol warrior as "tum." "Belly" won't cut it; "tummy" is a bit too precious. There's something perfect about "a pronounced stoutness about the tum," something so cheerfully bourgeois, it's endearing. It makes us want to give Mr. L.

Prosser a poke in the tum, just to watch him glare in indignation and straighten his little fur hat.

And then there's Arthur Dent himself, a singularly British protagonist; the accidental hero, polite and befuddled. As Zaphod Beeblebrox notes, his brain could easily be replaced with an electronic brain programmed to say, "What?" and "I don't understand," and "Where's the tea?" Poor Arthur's all reaction, trying to make sense of a nonsensical situation. When there's no sensible course of action, you might as well just lie down in the mud and hope the problem goes away.

The Hitchhiker's Guide to the Galaxy is not a profound work. More than anything, it makes us giggle. Douglas Adams has fun with his own country's national stereotypes and humanity's myriad foibles, but he does it with fondness. There's a palpable sense of glee to his absurdity. And there may be, along the way, a few things worth thinking about.

If I had to come up with a working theory about the sociohistorical roots of *The Hitchhiker's Guide*, I'd look to British colonialism. And if I were the academic literary theorist my old college professors hoped I'd become, I'd do research. I'd delve into the history of British colonists attempting to recreate a familiar societal structure in countries like India or Africa, where the existing culture was inimical to their efforts. I'd posit the notion that by Adams' time, the absurdity of such efforts had been absorbed into the collective unconscious of the nation. I'd do research in respected journals to find articles that backed up my supposition. And I would suggest that this recognition is the source of the absurdity that Douglas Adams seized and wrote large upon the galaxy, reenacting folly upon folly, with love and wit and humor; mostly humor.

Thankfully, I'm not.

And so, instead, I will settle for giggling at *The Hitchhiker's Guide*, for admiring Adams' ability to constantly surprise his readers and to convey so much in so little, and wondering why petunias are funnier than chrysanthemums. For wondering what in the world that long-ago businesswoman in staid attire was doing buying such a silly book, and whether she laughed out loud when she read it, or merely pursed her lips and nodded to herself in satisfied agreement. For wondering if the bookstore is still there on Fenchurch Street, and if she still shops there, and if she ever bought any of *my* books, and if she laughed out loud at any of the funny bits.

After all, they're there. It's just that they're…you know. Subtle.

Jacqueline Carey is the best-selling author of the critically acclaimed Kushiel's Legacy trilogy of historical fantasy novels and The Sundering epic fantasy duology. Jacqueline enjoys doing research on a wide variety of arcane topics, and an affinity for travel has taken her from Finland to Egypt to date. She currently lives in west Michigan, where she is a member of the oldest Mardi Gras krewe in the state. Although often asked by inquiring fans, she does not, in fact, have any tattoos.

Susan Sizemore

You Can't Go Home Again–Damn It! Even If Your Planet Hasn't Been Blown Up By Vogons

Susan Sizemore tries to go home and fails. She checks the map three times, and drives all around the neighborhood. She Googles for directions, checks information and knocks on people's doors—but she just can't go home. It's not her fault.

REALLY WISH I HADN'T taken this gig.

Let me explain. My introduction to Douglas Adams was late at night sometime back in the seventies. That was when I turned on the television to the sight of a curly-haired man in a long scarf hunting for something called the Key of Time in a hollowed-out planet and saying something like, "I'll never be cruel to an electron again." I goggled at this, laughed and settled down to watch the rest of the show. It was also my introduction to *Doctor Who*—but that's a subject for another essay. This *Doctor Who* episode was "The Pirate Planet" and was written by Douglas Adams. It sparked my addiction to the Doctor and to the work of this writer. I haven't seen *Doctor Who* in years, and I don't think I'm going to go back and watch them any time soon.

You see, when Glenn Yeffeth invited me to contribute to this book I was delighted. I thought I'd write an article about the influence *The Hitchhiker's Guide to the Galaxy* has had on my life. I have so many good memories of the events centered around the books, radio and television series, and Douglas Adams himself. I wanted to write an homage, so I delved back into my past.

I honestly do not remember whether I saw the series first, or read the books, or heard the album of the radio program first. I think it might have been the album. I do remember that the album was brought along by some new friends when they came for a visit way back in, well, I don't remember if it was the late seventies or early eighties. I remember that when we listened to the show it was awe-inspiringly brilliant, as all British comedy was to me at the time. Sharing *The Hitchhiker's Guide to the Galaxy* with friends was a great experience. Finding another thing in common strengthened a friendship that lasts until this day. In fact, I've collaborated on two books with one of these friends, and she has a much more serious article in this book. We still have *Hitchhiker's Guide* in common. So, thank you, Douglas Adams for that, as well as *Doctor Who*.

On other personal connections with the *Guide*—well, I did stalk Douglas Adams around the 1982 World Science Fiction Convention. Not exactly stalk. It was a sort of literary groupie thing. You see, Adams and my boyfriend were the two tallest people at the con, which made them easy to spot. My boyfriend spent most of his time in a Darth Vader costume. Douglas Adams was this fairly bewildered-looking pink-cheeked Englishman that another friend who also has an article in this book and I followed from panel to panel. We hung on his every word, though I do not recall what any of those words were now.

A year later, while rambling through the lovely Georgian streets of Bath, England, I noticed a handsome young man as he walked past, and I thought, "He's missing a head." I'm pretty sure that young man was Mark Wing-Davey, who played Zaphod Beeblebrox in the television series.

When I left my day job to become a full-time writer I left the message, "So long and thanks for all the fish" scrolling across the computer screen on my desk. And I knew that the engineers I'd worked with would get the reference.

And how many times over the years have I muttered, "He's just this guy, you know." Or, "Life. Don't talk to me about Life." Or, "The mice will see you now." Or any number of lines of wisdom from the *Guide*. While a lot of details faded with time, many remained firmly fixed in my brain.

My most surreal *Hitchhiker's Guide* moment came late in the morning on September 11, 2001, when I couldn't bear watching the television anymore and went out for a walk on that lovely clear day. I looked up at a sky that was the bluest I'd ever seen and watched the last couple of planes making their landing approach after all the airports had been shut down and flights cancelled. While watching the last planes into Minneapolis I recalled the Vogon Destructor Fleet and how, "The ships hung in the sky in much the same way that bricks don't."

I loved the television series. I memorized the series. And it turned out that I still remembered every word when I watched the DVD to begin my research. In fact, it was watching the show for the first time in nearly two decades that put me off the idea of writing this article. It was sooooo slooooooooowwwww. I was bored. Dear God, I was bored with *The Hitchhiker's Guide to the Galaxy!* Where was the snappy repartee I remembered? Where was the edgy social commentary? Not in the six episodes of the series. When I looked in the books I found them thin and plodding. I was devastated. They hadn't changed, but I had—and I couldn't relate to them anymore.

I seriously considered begging off doing the essay, because I didn't want to say the things I'm about to. But I'd already said I'd do it, and I honor my obligations. What I'd started out thinking was going to be an homage and an exercise in fond nostalgia turns out to be something else.

Because, upon a lot of thought about the reasons why, I have to admit that it's worse than boredom. I don't like *The Hitchhiker's Guide to the Galaxy* anymore. Not in any format. I'm as shocked as shocked can be. And I wish it weren't so.

While I recalled all the dialogue of the shows, there were a lot of things going on in them that I hadn't remembered. I'd forgotten how scathingly bitter the satire is in the television and radio versions. There are moments of sarcasm that are practically toxic. And what's with all this God stuff, anyway?

Yes, Douglas, God exists. It this relevant to humankind? Sometimes. Now, can we move on to really important things, like shoe sales and finding world peace for a few weeks without bringing God into it? I suppose I must have found the religious philosophizing amusing at one time; now I just find it heavy-handed and irritating.

I'm sure there's an essay somewhere in this book praising Adams' work as a timeless exploration of man's quest to find his place in the universe. Unfortunately, I find that opinion to be a total crock. At least the timeless part. I really hate realizing that time has passed *The Hitchhiker's Guide* by, at least for me. Because that is a big part of why I don't like it anymore. It hasn't aged well. I find it very much a product of the issues of the time and place it was created. If I still had any great nostalgia for the late seventies or early eighties I might not be so disappointed in reexamining *The Guide*.

For example, there's the whole thing about Trillian, the only significant female character until we get to *So Long and Thanks for All the Fish*, being the brains of the operation. Back then it was cute; now it's just outdated. All right, I realize that this is what Rowling does with Hermione in the *Harry Potter* books, but Rowling is deliberately being retro. Trillian was cutting-edge feminism for Adams. Shudder. Then there is Adams' heavy-handed concern for the growing materialism of the post-hippie early yuppie era as exemplified by human fascination with digital watches.

And calling someone the triple-breasted whore of somewhere isn't funny anymore. Titties are everywhere these days; a mention of them is not cool—except maybe to Ben Stiller or Adam Sandler, and I don't think they're funny, either. Okay, Stiller is when he isn't publicly humiliating himself.

And then there's the horror of Arthur's house being torn down by indifferent housing council bureaucrats in the name of progress. England was changing! And not for the better! How about that, Doug? I've spent a lot of time on English roads. Personally, I prefer modern British highways to quaint country lanes.

And then there's Zaphod representing the corruption, greed and stupidity of the scandal-ridden British government. That's government, for you. Yawn. Of course, we weren't quite as cynical then on either side of the Pond, though we were getting there.

What I think I've come to find the most cringe-worthy, dated part of the story is the class conscious snobbery disguised as satire of stranding dull, ordinary working people on a primitive planet simply because they are dull, ordinary working-class folk. Yes, they become our ancestors—but somehow Adams thought we should be ashamed of that. I'd rather be descended from a phone sanitizer, than, say, a Hilton sister.

There are notions in the books that I still love—Babel fish, the wretchedness of Vogon poetry, a themed restaurant that exploits the end of everything for entertainment, dolphins and the *Guide* itself among them. I never did like Arthur Dent much, but I pretended I did back in the day. I was a big Zaphod fan, but now I find him stupid. I still kind of like Ford. Okay, Marvin the robot is still funny, but Bender from Futurama could whomp his shiny metal ass any ol' time. Of course, there wouldn't be a Bender without Marvin. So I am grateful to the *Guide* for the influence it had on modern sf/f/comedy/satire.

Times change and tastes change. And for me, modern comedy leaves the *Guide* in the dust. I suppose the disenchantment started when I picked up my first Terry Pratchett book, though not on a conscious level, as such. At the time I do remember thinking, "This guy leaves Douglas Adams in the dust." I thought it, but I felt no interest in rereading Adams to compare. Having no interest in rereading Adams after being reminded of him by Pratchett should have been a clue. But, again, Pratchett's Discworld owes a debt to the groundbreaking work of Adams.

Perhaps with age I've come to prefer a kinder, gentler form of satire. These days I find that I prefer Bill and Ted's philosophy of being excellent to each other and partying on more important than knowing where my towel is. Adams' work was seminal, incredibly influential—But the *Hitchhiker's* universe moves at too slow a pace for my current humor needs. I do still rather like *So Long and Thanks for All the Fish*, because in the fourth book of the trilogy, Adams did get around to saving the world. That book has a hopeful ending. And I rather prefer hope to pessimism, at least in my fiction. Still, the humor in Adams doesn't scintillate anymore.

Heck, there was more hilarious political satire in the first five minutes of any Aaron Sorkin-penned episode of *West Wing* than in all of any version of the *Guide*. Then there's *Farscape*. When this show whips an everyman from Earth onto an alien spaceship, they make him funnier and tougher than Arthur Dent and his adventures far more relevant. The characters on *Futurama* are more engaging, and the sf satire is wonderfully witty on that Matt Groening-created animated series. The work of Trey Parker and Matt Stone is gross and juvenile, but wonderful. I want to wash out those swearing children on *South Parks'* mouths, but they still have some wise and witty things to say, and with frequent sf/f references.

I could go on, but it comes down to my not thinking that Adam's work stands the test of time. I've checked. Three out of four *Black Adders* are still funny (but I didn't like the fourth one to begin with). So is *Red Dwarf*. *Monty Python's Flying Circus* remain works of mad genius. So it's not just that I'm no longer thrilled by British humor. It's that I should have left *The Hitchhiker's Guide* in the good memory vault. Like I said at the beginning, I wish I hadn't taken this gig.

However, there's a *Hitchhiker's Guide* movie in the works. I have hopes that a modern updating and revamping of what's still a great premise will revive my love of the *Guide*. So, Douglas Adams, thank you for introducing me to the Doctor, thanks for all the great dialogue. Thank you for influencing decades of sf/f humor. And so long, and thanks for all the fish.

In the meantime, I am definitely not going to be watching any old *Doctor Who* episodes anytime soon. That's a long-standing love affair I am not willing to end.

Media junkie Susan Sizemore is the author of numerous novels and short stories, ranging from historical romance to epic fantasy. She has an affinity for vampire fiction, basketball, coffee canines and movies with explosions. For more information, Susan's Web site address is http://susansizemore.com.

Vox Day

The Subversive Dismal Scientist: Douglas Adams and the Rule of Unreason

It's a little-known fact that Douglas Adams was close friends with Nobel Prize-winning economist Milton Friedman, whom he met while obtaining his doctorate in economics at the University of Chicago. An advisor and confidant to Margaret Thatcher, he was responsible for much of Thatcher's economic platform, and was instrumental in her rise to power. Actually no. None of that was true. But it could have been....

I T IS NOT WRITTEN IN THIRTY-FOOT-HIGH LETTERS of fire on top of the Quentulus Quazgar Mountains, but there is a distinct message that can be found woven throughout Douglas Adams' (regrettably no longer) increasingly inaccurately named Hitchhiker's Trilogy. His is a seditious message, a wildly subversive one, in fact, considering the ironic circumstances of its germination and subsequent propagation.

The dark master of the black art of humor, Adams is a fearless thrower of flames; an equal-opportunity mocker, his targets are freely distributed across the spectrum. He ridicules rock bands, religious fundamentalists, quantum mechanists, environmentalists and the *Oxford English Dictionary*. He mocks Hollywood screenwriters and philosophers with equal enthusiasm; he lampoons politicians and poets with effortlessly cruel flair. If an author can be discerned through the veil of his characters, he would appear to be more Wowbagger the Infinitely Prolonged than the long-suffering Arthur Dent, though Adams does not trouble to order his taunts alphabetically.

To fully appreciate the overarching contempt that fuels Adams' humor, it is necessary to understand that the government that inspired it was not the post-Thatcher New Labour of Tony Blair's Cool Britannia, but the grim, ponderous Old Labour regime of Harold Wilson and James Callaghan. Economically illiterate and dominated by socialist trade unions, its policies had led to a severe devaluation of the pound combined with harsh currency controls that limited the amount of cash British vacationers could take out of the country, forcing a nation with colonies in Bermuda and the Virgin Islands to spend its vacations at the cold Atlantic beaches of Blackpool.

The Hitchhiker's Guide to the Galaxy begins with the indelible image of a showdown between a bulldozer and a man futilely attempting to defend his property against the proclaimed interest of the governing authorities. The remorseless and inexorable logic of the Council—you've got to build bypasses—was recently echoed in the U.S. by the Connecticut Supreme Court, which ruled that the city of New London was operating within its rights when it used its power of eminent domain to condemn the middle-class Fort Trumbull neighborhood in order to permit developers to knock down ninety homes and replace them with upscale condominiums and an office park.

One hopes that unlike the case of Arthur Dent's house, these demolitions will not soon be followed by the total destruction of the Earth.

This classic critique of eminent domain is far from the only one that Adams makes in his clandestine litany of the mindless abuses of government. His feelings on the bureaucrats who run the show could hardly be made more clear when he writes that it is the ugly, unevolved Vogons who have migrated in mass to the political hub of the galaxy and now make up "the immensely powerful backbone of the Galactic Civil Service." Anyone who has had the misfortune of encountering the corpulent troglodytes who dwell in department of transportation offices will readily recognize where Adams likely found his inspiration for both the Vogon's appearance and their unhelpful philosophy.

They are one of the most unpleasant races in the Galaxy—not actually evil, but bad tempered, bureaucratic, officious and callous. They wouldn't even lift a finger to save their own grandmothers from the Ravenous Bugblatter Beast of Traal without orders signed in triplicate, sent in, sent back, queried, lost, found, subjected to public inquiry, lost again, and finally buried in soft peat and recycled as firelighters.[1]

This profoundly negative attitude toward government is not limited to observations of its low-level functionaries, but is instead a broad-based, highly conceptual worldview. The citizen of a world-spanning empire declining into global irrelevance, Douglas Adams paints a picture of a galaxy in similar decline, where the "wild, rich and largely tax-free" days of glory and greatness are lost in the mists of time and those who cater to the wealthy Galactic elite are forced to hibernate in time stasis to wait until the economic cycle of boom and bust plays itself out.

Remarkably, Adams manages to mine this unlikely field, economics, for some of his most scathing barbs. The dismal science does not often figure into fictional plot lines and still less is it played for laughs, but nevertheless, it has an integral role in both the overall story and Adams' underlying theme. Indeed, Adams betrays a remarkably sophisticated understanding of economics when he pokes fun at the Marxian concept of capitalist crisis in the Shoe Event Horizon that ruins the world of Frogstar World B. Furthermore, his grasp of the dangers of inflation is not only markedly superior to the world's current central bankers, but he also lays the blame squarely where it lies, namely, with the government authorities responsible for adopting an inherently worthless paper currency subject to inevitable inflation.

---

[1] *The Hitchhiker's Guide to the Galaxy*, p. 47

"Thank you. Since we decided a few weeks ago to adopt the leaf as legal tender, we have, of course, all become immensely rich."

Ford stared in disbelief at the crowd who were murmuring appreciatively at this and greedily fingering the wads of leaves with which their track suits were stuffed.

"But we have also," continued the Management Consultant, "run into a small inflation problem on account of the high level of leaf availability, which means that, I gather, the current going rate has something like three deciduous forests buying one ship's peanut."

Murmurs of alarm came from the crowd. The Management Consultant waved them down.

"So in order to obviate this problem," he continued, "and effectively revaluate the leaf, we are about to embark on a massive defoliation campaign, and...er, burn down all the forests. I think you'll all agree that's a sensible move under the circumstances."[2]

It would seem that the British government's currency disaster of his youth left an indelible impression on Adams, for he mentions the collapse of the Altairan dollar on more than one occasion and expresses deep skepticism about the concept of compound interest outpacing inflation in describing how one pays for a meal at Milliways, the restaurant at the end of the universe, with a single penny. Indeed, Adams' environmentalist take on paper currency sounds very much like the Austrian School economist Murray Rothbard, whose seminal history of money and banking chronicles how American monetary authorities have repeatedly caused social and economic calamity through an addiction to expansive monetary policy:

The issue of this fiat "Continental" paper rapidly escalated over the next few years.... The result was, as could be expected, a rapid price inflation in terms of the paper notes, and a corollary accelerating depreciation of the paper in terms of specie [gold or silver coin]. Thus, at the end of 1776, the Continentals were worth $1 to $1.25 in specie; by the fall of the following year, its value had fallen to 3-to-1; by December 1778 the value was 6.8-to-1; and by December 1779, to the negligible 42-to-1. By the spring of 1781, the Continentals were virtually worthless, exchanging on the market at 168 dollars to one dollar

---

[2]*The Restaurant at the End of the Universe*, p. 204

in specie. This collapse of the Continental currency gave rise to the phrase "not worth a Continental."[3]

Money mismanagement is far from the only form of gross government incompetence targeted by Adams. When Marvin is stuck in the swamp on Squornshellous Zeta, the robot tells a mattress named Zem about a speech he once gave at the opening of a thousand-mile bridge constructed in the swamp. "It was going to revitalize the economy of the Squornshellous System," he informs the flolloping Zem. "They spent the entire economy of the Squornshellous System building it."[4]

Friedrich Hayek's "Two Pages of Fiction: The Impossibility of Socialist Calculation," is famous for demonstrating how the central planner's task is bound to be a hopeless one, but Adams takes the concept one step further by pointing out the inevitable absurdities as well. Squornshellous Zeta's economic revival project fails in a spectacular manner at what should have been its moment of glory by sinking into the swamp and killing everyone. In addition to being a critique of central planning, this vignette could also be seen as a sly reference to the lethal nature of socialist governments in the twentieth century, which so often began by promising Heaven on Earth and instead delivered Hell.

Adams exposes the fundamental flaw at the heart of all centralism in the defeat of the murderous xenophobes of Krikkit, whose legions of deadly white robots operate under the direct control of the Krikkit War Computer. In much the same way that the Mongols, on the verge of conquering Europe in 1242, were brought to a complete halt by the death of Ogedai Khan, the Krikkit war machine is shut down by the exposure of the War Computer's central intelligence core to the suicidally depressed robot. It is worth noting that Adams again ties together the concepts of centralism and mass death, as the Clerk of the Court at the War Crimes Trial concludes that two grillion guys were "zilched out" by the forces of Krikkit.

In addition to his unexpectedly fruitful harvest in the comedic orchards of death, war crimes and monetary policy, Adams manages to find hilarity in the always amusing topic of taxes. He jabs effectively at static revenue models (which assert that individual behavior will remain the same despite changing tax rates), by introducing Arthur Dent to the corpse of Disaster Area lead singer Hotblack Desiato, who is "spending

---

[3] Murray Rothbard, *A History of Money and Banking in the United States*, p. 59.

[4] *Life, The Universe and Everything*, p. 58.

the year dead for tax reasons," and in doing so, highlights how government policies force otherwise rational humans to behave in an irrational manner.

Other government-fostered irrationalities are exposed in the brief discussion of bad poetry following Arthur and Ford's escape from Earth. While the execrable and oft deadly Vogon poetry is a natural artifact of Vogon culture, public funding results in an even more dangerous form of composition:

> The second worst is that of the Azagoths of Kria. During a recitation by their Poet Master Grunthos the Flatulent of his poem "Ode To A Small Lump of Green Putty I Found In My Armpit One Midsummer Morning" four of his audience died of internal hemorrhaging, and the President of the Mid-Galactic Arts Nobbling Council survived by gnawing one of his own legs off.[5]

The savage irony of The Hitchhiker's Guide to the Galaxy, what is surely Douglas Adams' greatest and most subtle joke, is that this overtly anti-government collection of subversion was not only funded by the British government, but distributed by it to the masses in a variety of formats through the BBC. Through Hitchhiker's, Douglas Adams does not so much bite the hand that was feeding him as rip it off entirely, leaving nothing but a bloody stump behind. The dichotomy is almost precisely the reverse of Lenin's famous construction; in this case, the socialist state gave the very rope to the writer with which he throttled it.

Adams' theme cannot honestly be characterized as a Thatcherite one—his interests ran more toward pointing out problems and contradictions than proposing policies to address them—but even so, it appears to be more than a coincidence that the first airing of the Hitchhiker's radio program should have been March 8, 1978, five weeks after a massive nationwide strike by the four major public service unions and a scant eight weeks before the British people threw the Labour Party out of office following seventeen ruinous years of post-war dominance. It seems logical to conclude that the conservative wave which swept Britain and brought Margaret Thatcher to power also helped in establishing Douglas Adams as a worldwide literary star.

Certainly, Britain's new Prime Minister must have approved of his take on trade unions. The concept of a philosopher's union is humorous

---

[5]The Hitchhiker's Guide to the Galaxy, p. 59

enough in itself, but Adams' adept description of how unions use the government's legal muscle to reinforce their position to stifle technological advancement teaches more in a paragraph than most elite economics courses can manage in a semester in describing how corrupt power politics are used to inhibit entrepeneurship and economic growth.

It is unfortunate that Douglas Adams is now seen primarily as an amusing writer of science fiction. He was much more than that. The five books of the Hitchhiker's trilogy are, in their own unique manner, every bit as serious and as provokingly philosophical as Voltaire's *Candide* or Jonathan Swift's *A Modest Proposal*. Douglas Adams may not have been a Libertarian, but his works deserve to be categorized among the most powerfully libertarian literature to have ever seen print.

But the anti-government theme of The Hitchhiker's Guide to the Galaxy can best be summarized in Adams' own words, which leave little doubt as to the author's deep skepticism with regard to the rational nature and reasonable intentions of those who seek to rule over their fellow man.

The major problem—one of the major problems, for there are several—one of the many major problems with governing people is that of whom you get to do it; or rather of who manages to get people to let them do it to them. To summarize: it is a well known fact, that those people who most want to rule people are, ipso facto, those least suited to do it. To summarize the summary: anyone who is capable of getting themselves made President should on no account be allowed to do the job.[6]

Vox Day is a nationally syndicated political columnist and fantasy author. He has published four novels with Pocket Books as well as three graphic novels, and was a founder of the award-winning techno band Psykosonik. He maintains a popular blog, Vox Popoli, and is an active member of the Science Fiction and Fantasy Writers Association.

[6]*The Restaurant at the End of the Universe*, p. 175

Stephen Baxter

Lunching at the Eschaton: Douglas Adams and the End of the Universe in Science Fiction

Science fiction had taken us to the end of the universe before Adams did, but Adams was the first to open a restaurant there. Adams took the tropes of science fiction and gave them a twist that was often both comic and insightful—talking animals that offered you a meal of their bodies, intelligent robots with attitudes problems and speaking appliances that were irritatingly cheerful.

Adams took in the genre's best ideas and then gave them back to us, but with a comic twist. Acclaimed science fiction author Stephen Baxter explains

N ONE OF THE MOST MEMORABLE and comic sequences in the Hitchhiker's Guide to the Galaxy saga, Douglas Adams visits the end of the universe to open a restaurant: "If the lady and gentlemen would care to take drinks before dinner...the Universe will explode later for your pleasure" [1] (chapter fourteen).

But Adams was not the first science fictional visitor to the "eschaton,"the end of everything—nor will he be the last. And *The Restaurant at the End of the Universe* helped shape a tradition of end-of-everything fiction that continues to this day.

The science of eschatology was born in the nineteenth century with the notion of entropy, inflicted on us in 1850 by Rudolf Clausius. The dread Second Law of Thermodynamics dictates that global entropy must increase to a maximum—that is, energy sources such as stars must gradually run down, and the free energy available for life must then necessarily dwindle. The far future of the universe and humankind, increasingly starved of energy by this "Heat Death," looked bleak indeed.

In 1895 H. G. Wells memorably explored this dismal new prospect in *The Time Machine* [2]. The Time Traveller, having escaped the Morlocks, journeys into the future, "drawn on by the mystery of the earth's fate," until he reaches a time thirty million years hence, when a swollen sun has obliterated all traces of man and his works. Life is gone, apart from a green slime on the rocks, and "a black object flopping about" on a sandbank.

Later, writers such as Olaf Stapledon [3], Isaac Asimov[4] and Arthur C. Clarke [5] considered the end of the universe in their own science fiction, and in many of their works, unsurprisingly, a quest for God is key. A computer is used to analyze holy writings in Clarke's famous end-of-the-world story "The Nine Billion Names of God" (1953) [5], in which, "overhead, without any fuss, the stars were going out."

Stapledon's 1937 classic *Star Maker* [3] is all about this quest for God. The unnamed protagonist, a man living somewhere outside London, is lifted out of his here and now and transported on a stunning psychical journey through the cosmos. At first the wandering mind is attracted to worlds similar to Earth. But eventually he witnesses the birth and death of the cosmos as a whole, and at last the united mind of the dying cosmos sets out in search of the Star Maker, the organizing spirit that transcends creation. In a sequence of staggering invention that pre-echoes writers like Greg Egan, we are shown how the universe is but one of an infinite "hypercosmical" series of creations. But the universes are "bright but trivial bubbles," their only purpose to enable the Star Maker itself to grow.

When God became more difficult to find, some authors allowed their characters to create him themselves. In Isaac Asimov's 1956 story "The Last Question" [4], two drunken technicians, arguing about the death of the sun, ask the world-spanning computer Multivac the ultimate question: "How can the net amount of entropy in the universe be massively decreased?" After much flashing of lights and clicking of relays (this was 1956), the answer comes: "INSUFFICIENT DATA FOR MEANINGFUL ANSWER." The question is posed to Multivac's descendants, again and again as history unfolds, and finally, after ten trillion years, by the last independent mind before its fusion with Multivac—or AC, as it has become. AC thinks it over and figures out what to do. "And AC said, 'Let there be light!' And there was light—" This is a lift of the finest sound bite in the Bible, of course, and the feel-good ending has made "The Last Question" one of Asimov's most popular stories (indeed, his own favorite).

Despite the presence of earlier eschatalogical science fiction, Adams might not have been strongly affected by it. In fact, Adams' knowledge of science fiction is a matter of debate among his biographers [6]. Did Adams read "The Last Question," for instance? Perhaps; AC reads like a prototype for Deep Thought. But the story seems unlikely to have influenced Adams' thinking directly. He once said rather unkindly of Asimov, "I wouldn't employ him to write junk mail" [6].

Adams seems to have been a "reader" rather than a "fan," not an expert on the literature and its subculture. As a boy he read juvenile science fiction, such as by W. E. Johns and the *Eagle* comic (Dan Dare), and later enjoyed the works of Robert Sheckley, Philip K. Dick, Robert Silverberg, Kurt Vonnegut and others. But of H. G. Wells he said, "I've read *The War of the Worlds* and *The Time Machine*, but I can't remember them making a great impression on me." And even of Clarke: "His writing is a little dull perhaps." [6] Surely his subconscious soaked up the concepts and the best of the material, but it's hard to imagine Douglas Adams taking seriously the doom-laden graveness of some sf writers.

Perhaps more significant in shaping Adams' thinking about the end of the world was his own religious background. Adams was brought up as a committed and reflective Christian. Later in life, though, he began to believe that religious thinking conflicted with a scientific worldview. Eventually he fell under the spell of Richard Dawkins, the strong-viewed evolutionary biologist, and began to describe himself as a radical atheist. Some of his friends mused that had he lived he would have resolved this conflict and come to some synthesis of belief.

The trouble with giving up Christianity is that the end of the world suddenly seems a much bleaker prospect. In Christendom, the New Testament had taught us that the future is finite: that the world will, inevitably, end. But we were able to console ourselves with the belief that we would live on in God, beyond the end of the world and into eternity. Now, thanks to science, we had to believe that the universe is doomed to expire, in fire or darkness, taking us, our descendants and all our works with it. And without God, without an afterlife, what consolation is there?

Instead of the graveness of Stapledon and Asimov, Adams' response to finding himself adrift in a vast and pitiless universe seems to have been much more influenced by the absurdist humor of Robert Sheckley and, especially, Kurt Vonnegut—not to mention Monty Python and Lewis Carroll: "If you've done six impossible things this morning, why not round it off with breakfast at Milliways, the Restaurant at the End of the Universe?" (chapter fifteen) is a very Carrollian line.

Adams looks cosmic doom in the face and laughs. He neatly pokes fun at religion's eschatological uselessness when the Great Prophet Zarquon messes up his second coming by arriving in Milliways just seconds before the end of the universe (chapter eighteen). And Adams is well aware of the apparent futility of all action given the finitude of time. Milliways' oleaginous host Max Quordlepleen tells his audience, "I know that so many of you come here time and time again...to come and watch this final end of everything, and then return home to your own eras...and raise families, strive for new and better societies, fight terrible wars for what you know to be right....It really gives one hope for the future of all life-kind. Except, of course, that we know it hasn't got one..." (chapter seventeen).

Life is meaningless: after all the central joke of the entire *Hitchhiker* sequence is that Earth is actually a computer constructed to help resolve the meaning of life, and when in ignorance and arrogance the planet is destroyed to make room for a bypass, all hope of finding such meaning disappears. But Adams, even while despairing, laughs at it all.

Compare and contrast Adams with the physicist Steven Weinberg, who once remarked dolefully, "It is very hard to realize that [Earth] is just a tiny part of an overwhelmingly hostile Universe....The more the Universe seems comprehensible, the more it seems pointless" [7]. Weinberg is most famous for chronicling the other end of the universe: the first three minutes after the Big Bang. The Big Bang? Douglas Adams put a Burger Bar there where Max Quordlepleen hosts another nightly show (chapter seventeen).

And, perhaps, by showing us how to laugh at cosmic ruin, Adams shaped the eschatological science fiction that followed.

Science fiction is generally a literature of action, of possibilities. Do we have to lie down and take this Heat Death business? Or is there a way out?

The first serious modern attempt to answer to such questions was made by the Princeton physicist Freeman Dyson, who in 1979—a year before the book version of *Restaurant* was published—delivered a landmark series of lectures on the far future [8]. Dyson sketched, complete with numerical estimates, the far future of a universe which continues to expand and the types of physical processes that might prevail.

Dyson's philosophy was essentially optimistic; he sought to demonstrate that as far ahead as it was possible to look the universe would continue to evolve. Long after the death of the stars, for example, the night sky will be illuminated by such gigantic events as the explosion of black holes. Still, the dead hand of the Second Law will hold overall sway, as available energy sources diminish. Dyson, however, demonstrated that it ought to be possible, in principle at least, for an intelligence to extract an infinite amount of experience—counted as changes in state, "thoughts"—from a finite amount of energy, perhaps by enduring long periods of dreamless hibernation. But survival seems to depend on the outcome of a race between the gathering of energy sources and their dissipation by entropy—a race humans may be doomed to lose [9].

Whether this prospect—of an increasingly heroic battle by our no-longer-human descendants to maintain life and consciousness in a dwindling universe—is dismal or uplifting depends on your point of view. Still, Dyson's notions evoked many responses in science fiction.

Frederik Pohl's 1990 novel *The World at the End of Time* [10] is the story of an interstellar colony world arbitrarily dragged on a high-speed traverse across the universe by a petulant, paranoid, star-dwelling creature called Wan-To. The human protagonist, Viktor, is hopped forward through time thanks to a mix of cryogenic freezing and relativistic time dilation, while the universe through which his world speeds ages hundreds of billions of years. In the end Wan-To submits to entropy, the most powerful of creatures suspended in the dismal energy-starved far future like Judas in Dante's ice: "[Wan-To] was trapped. He was embedded in a nearly solid mass, like a man buried in sand up to his neck...."

The endless expansion of an open universe is not the only possibility, of course. Perhaps we live in a *closed* universe—that is, a future in which the universe eventually ceases its expansion and collapses back to a "Big Crunch," a time-reversed rerun of the Big Bang. At first glance the prospect of being Crunched out of existence seems even more unbearable than expanding into oblivion: Freeman Dyson remarked [8] that a closed universe gave him "a feeling of claustrophobia, to imagine our whole Universe confined within a box." Could we physically survive such a devastating terminus?

This question was explored in George Zebrowski's 1979 novel *Macrolife* [11], which takes its title from the idea of large communities of sentient beings, traveling between the stars in giant free-floating habitats, which become a form of life in their own right—macrolife, a life more than the sum of its parts. After giant leaps through time to one hundred billion years hence, macrolife—by now a universe-spanning community of many species—faces imminent extinction as the universe collapses. The book's climactic scene, of the macrolife worlds hurtling around the all-devouring black hole at the end of time, is exhilarating and chilling.

In 1994 the science caught up with the fiction when physicist Frank Tipler gave eschatological optimists their greatest fillip to date. Tipler [12] demonstrated, at least to his own satisfaction, that it would be possible for future intelligences to manipulate the final collapse—essentially causing the universe to oscillate wildly—to provide an energy source that would, at the final eschaton, become *infinite*. And with this infinite energy it would be possible to think an infinite number of thoughts, to have an infinite number of experiences and so to achieve eternal life, even in a finite time.

Tipler speculated further that perhaps the giant end-of-time computing machines would be able (in fact, would be *bound*) to recreate in exact detail every sentient being in the universe's long history. Tipler claimed this would amount to a literal resurrection—not of a *copy* of you, but a *resurrection* of you—at the end of time. It is almost as if Asimov's AC may come to pass [4].

So one day you may indeed be reborn at the end of the universe, where you will find not just every restaurant that ever existed, but Deep Thought too. Book your table at Milliway's now.

To say the least, not all physicists—and even fewer theologians—agreed with Tipler's conclusions. But, flawed or not, compared to Dyson's dismal frozen-in-time scenario, Tipler's future is bright and glittering. It's not surprising that Tipler's notions had an almost immediate impact on science fiction.

In Frederik Pohl's *The Other End of Time* [13] Earth is caught up in a vast interstellar war in which one set of protagonists is actually motivated by their faith in Tipler's eschaton; they believe that murder is a mere fast-forwarding of the victim to resurrection in high-tech heaven. In *Tomorrow and Tomorrow* [14], Charles Sheffield's characters actually attempt to reach the Tipler eschaton. Drake Merlin's wife Ana has contracted a ferocious cancer. Drake has her frozen as a cryocorpse, hoping to see her revived in the future, when medical technology will have advanced sufficiently to cure her. In the end Drake has to project himself and Ana ever deeper into time, using relativistic time dilation, electronic downloading and other time-evading tricks. After billions of years Drake—now a universe-spanning composite—sets off on the final leg of his journey to the end of time itself, where his wife is revived by a Tiplerian computer-god.

The latest cosmological theories, however, indicate we live in an ever-expanding universe, not a contracting one. There will be no Big Crunch and no Tiplerian Deep Thought at the end of time. But end-of-the-universe science fiction continues to be written; I went there myself in my novel *Time* [15] (and gave a fuller review of the field in an earlier essay [16]).

So, interestingly, *Restaurant* stands at a crossroads in the eschatological tradition, when a poetic acceptance of cosmic doom gave way to a determination to find some way to survive. Dyson's 1979 synthesis of the far future was surely the primary inspiration for the new wave of works, but some authors surely drew strength from Douglas Adams' bold nose-thumbing response to the cosmic conclusion.

Adams' humor helped demythologize a rather dismal trope: we don't have to accept the end of things, and if we can laugh at it, maybe we can do something about it.

There is a dark, bleak aspect to Douglas Adams' humor, which certainly comes to the fore in later books, but is perhaps epitomized by the central joke of *Restaurant*: that cosmic doom can be colonized by caterers.

Adams' fiction sometimes reads as if he had been exposed to one of his own creations, the Total Perspective Vortex, in which you see "in one instant the whole infinity of creation and [yourself] in relation to it" (Chapter eleven). This annihilates the brains of Vortex users, for "if life is going to exist in a universe of this size, then the one thing it cannot afford to have is a sense of proportion." But Adams survived the Vortex, by laughing at the absurdity of it all—even of the final doom of everything.

As Max Quordlepleen says, (chapter seventeen), "After [the end of the Universe] there is nothing. Void. Emptiness. Oblivion. Absolutely nothing. Nothing... except of course for the sweet trolley, and a fine selection of Aldebaran liqueurs!"" And if we can laugh, we can hope. "Listen, forget it," says Ford Prefect in *Restaurant*'s last chapter (thirty-four), "forget all of it. Nothing matters. Look, it's a beautiful day, enjoy it."

Douglas Adams may have been influenced by the doom-laden eschatological fiction that went before him, and *Restaurant* surely influenced the more constructive works that followed. Perhaps more importantly, however, *Restaurant* contains (in my opinion) the best joke in the Hitchhiker's Guide sequence: Milliways, the eponymous eatery itself. Perhaps this is why *Restaurant* was Adams' own favorite of his Hitchhiker books [6].

The eschaton deserves nothing less.

Stephen Baxter was born in Liverpool, England, in 1957. He is a Chartered Engineer. He applied to become a cosmonaut in 1991—aiming for the guest slot on *Mir* eventually taken by Helen Sharman—but fell at an early hurdle. His first professionally published short story appeared in 1987, and his science fiction novels have been published in the UK, the US and in many other countries. His most recent books include *Exultant* (Del Rey 2005), part of a series called Destiny's Children; and *Time's Eye* (Del Rey 2004), the first of a new collaborative series with Sir Arthur C. Clarke called A Time Odyssey.

References

[1] Douglas Adams, *The Restaurant at the End of the Universe*, London 1980. Chapter numbers from the 1980 Pan Books edition.
[2] H. G. Wells, *The Time Machine*, London 1985.
[3] Olaf Stapledon, *Star Maker*, London 1937.
[4] Isaac Asimov, "The Last Question," *Science Fiction Quarterly*, 1956.
[5] Arthur C. Clarke, "The Nine Billion Names of God," *Star Science Fiction Stories*, 1953.
[6] MJ Simpson, *Hitchhiker: A Biography of Douglas Adams*, London, 2003.
[7] Steven Weinberg, *The First Three Minutes*, New York 1977.
[8] Freeman Dyson, "'Time Without End: Physics and Biology in an Open Universe," *Review of Modern Physics* vol. 51, pp 447-60, 1979.
[9] Steven Frautschi, "Entropy in an Expanding Universe," *Science*, vol. 217 pp 593-599, 1982.
[10] Frederik Pohl, *The World at the End of Time*, New York 1990.
[11] George Zebrowski, *Macrolife*, New York 1979.
[12] Frank Tipler, *The Physics Of Immortality*, New York, 1994.
[13] Frederik Pohl, *The Other End of Time*, New York, 1996.
[14] Charles Sheffield, *Tomorrow and Tomorrow*, New York 1997.
[15] Stephen Baxter, *Manifold 1: Time*, London 1999.
[16] Stephen Baxter, *Omegatropic*, London, 2001 .

A. M. Dellamonica

Digital Watches May Be a Pretty Neat Idea, But Peanuts and Beer Are What Get You Through the Apocalypse

Adams wasn't always obsessed with food. Sometimes he was obsessed with drink.

IMAGINE *THE HITCHHIKER'S GUIDE TO THE GALAXY* and its sequels without food and drink.

Easy, right?

Oh, sure, you'd have to go back in time and get Douglas Adams to cut that utterly fabulous scene at the core of *The Restaurant at the End of the Universe*, where the Dish of the Day tries to sell Arthur a nice bit of his shoulder before going off to shoot himself...and promising to do it humanely. In fact, Adams would have to cut out the whole restaurant. And maybe re-title the book.

But that wouldn't be such a big deal, would it? Other than that one teeny little thing, the rest would all be more or less the same, right?

Okay, perhaps there may be one or two other cosmetic changes. Like tea. Remember Arthur Dent describing tea in lavishly sensual terms to the Nutri-Matic Drinks Synthesizer, tying up the shipboard computer in the process and almost getting everyone aboard the *Heart of Gold* killed? Come to that, wasn't tea integral to the invention of the *Heart of Gold*'s Infinite Improbability Drive? And what about all the delicious food-related throwaway details—the way Arthur, when he's trying to grasp the wholly ungraspable notion that the Earth is destroyed, seizes on the idea that there is no longer such a thing as a McDonald's hamburger? Not to mention the way every planet in the Galaxy has a completely different drink whose name sounds like "gin and tonic."

And say, now that we've cleverly eased over to the subject of alcohol, let's try imagining a Hitchhiker's Guide to the Galaxy series without Pan Galactic Gargle Blasters.

What's that, you say? Sacrilege?

I couldn't agree more.

Douglas Adams' Hitchhiker's series is simply crammed with references to food and drink. Arthur's escape from Earth begins with a trip to the pub with Ford Prefect for beer and peanuts. His last visit to Earth comes to its sudden and devastating end in a nightclub. And where Arthur goes, the Galaxy follows: no great cosmic event—be it the Big Bang or the End of the Universe—is complete without a dining experience attached to it.

Food in this series is far more than nutrition. It is an engine that drives science. Not only does tea, as mentioned, summon the Infinite Improbability Drive from thin air, Bistromathics—a form of chaos theory based on diner interactions within a small restaurant—powers Slartibartfast's even faster *Starship Bistromath*. And, just as it has since the earliest days of human civilization, food products also serve as a form of primitive medicine. The pub food Ford procures for Arthur before their journey begins is therapeutic—cushioning his system before matter transference, and supplying protein and salt after. Later, a meal of unidentifiable moldy things from Arthur's fridge kills a virulent space disease he doesn't even know he's carrying. Drink is a cure in its own right, too, easing the psychic anguish felt by Ford and Zaphod Beeblebrox on any number of occasions.

Here and there over the course of the series, food even comes to be imbued with religious significance. Arthur reflects on rubbery English sandwiches and how they are an atonement for sin in *So Long, and Thanks for All the Fish*. Meanwhile, gratitude for fishy offerings is what motivates the dolphins when they decide to bring the Earth back into existence, resurrecting it like Lazarus after the Vogons trash it.

After he journeys far and wide across the cosmos, losing the woman he loves in the process, Arthur settles down on an Earthlike planet. There he finally achieves happiness and inner peace by becoming a sandwich-maker.

But what does it all mean? Why are these books crammed to overflowing with snacks, drinking binges, restaurant trips, references to tea and plain old hunger? Why would Adams spend so much time and text on something as ordinary as food when he could instead have been giving readers another chase scene, or some witty Ford-Zaphod banter?

The answer is simple: Arthur's relationship with food is a constant reminder that that he is an ordinary human being, that he is just like us. At the same time, it helps readers understand his state of mind throughout the amazing and improbable journey that is his life.

When we are first introduced to Arthur, he's described as a thirty-year-old who "is never quite at ease with himself." Just a few pages later, he learns that aliens from outer space are real, deadly and sometimes green. As if that revelation wasn't enough for one day—heck, for one lifetime—he has only just escaped the total destruction of his homeworld. Everything he knows is gone—house, family, neighborhood pub—and he is given no better reason than "You've got to build bypasses."

The destruction of Earth is even more tragic because it is so utterly pointless, and if Douglas Adams had been writing a dramatic tear-jerking angst-ridden work of fiction—the sort of thing that sits at the front of bookstores, covered in gold stickers announcing the many literary awards the author has won—then he might have comfortably gone on for pages about Arthur's sense of loss and his survivor guilt. Then he could have turned his and our attention on the castaway's frustrated desire to return home. There's so much death, loss and suffering in these books, after all, that there would have been plenty of grist to keep the litany of sorrow going. In anyone else's hands, in fact, the Hitchhiker's series would be positively morbid, the sort of thing one reads—to get in the mood—just before jumping off a bridge.

Luckily for us all, though, *The Hitchhiker's Guide to the Galaxy* is a comedy...and that kind of extended mopefest just doesn't fit in with the general tone of the series.

Still. You can hardly exterminate your protagonist's home planet and expect him not to notice, can you?

So as Arthur Dent struggles with an unimaginable disaster and copes with his unfolding adventures with Ford, we see him constantly brushing up against the most fundamental of human needs: the pressing need to figure out where his next meal is coming from.

But before we begin to track Arthur's journey through space, time and probability—not to mention a goodly number of restaurants—it might be a good idea to talk about how hungry humans in general tackle the same biological imperative.

Humanity's relationship with food was at one time pretty simple. A person had to ingest enough nutrients in a day to see him through to the next sunrise. That was it. If you could root it up, pick it off the bushes or kill it with a pointy stick, you got to eat it...which in turn meant you got to live. At least, you did if whatever it was you'd harvested didn't turn out to be toxic in some way.

The dangers were legion. Any meal might be rotten, filled with parasites or naturally poisonous. Take almonds, for example. They seem innocent enough when you find them in the supermarket, but wild almonds are vicious creatures bent on poisoning anyone who gets near them. Their seeds are laced with a bitter-tasting chemical called amygdalin, which when ingested breaks down into cyanide. Then consider the inconvenient fact that meat products come from animals, many of which would be only too happy to bite, gore or trample a hungry hunter-gatherer to death if given a good reason and half a chance.

So after a while the root, pick and pointy-stick diet went out of style and humans developed farming, supermarkets, pizza delivery and four-star dining. Suddenly millions of humans have access to the small green pieces of paper and plastic that make it possible to eat three square meals a day without risking death at the claws of an angry wounded tiger.

As our day-to-day lives got further and further from a struggle for subsistence, our relationship with food got increasingly complex. By the late seventies, when Douglas Adams wrote the first Hitchhiker's novel, humans in wealthy countries were regularly navigating a nutritional maze packed with food fashions, diet fads, vitamins, supervitamins, eating disorders, organic produce, fast food, slow food, instant mashed potatoes and even juice bars that reduce fruits, vegetables and wheat grass to green, drinkable slime.

Now, ironically, many of us are so far removed from the cornfield or the salmon run that we could not even grow our own food if we lacked the money to buy it. Forget for a second that most of us don't know how. Farmland is too scarce and expensive, for one thing. And agricultural technology has moved unbelievably far from the old paradigm whereby one would plow a field, plant it and commence praying for rain.

Consider a time-honored and cost-saving farming technique like saving seed from last year's crop to plant the following spring. This is something humans have been doing for thousands of years—but now it is also sometimes against the law. This is because many food plants are patented, making it illegal to germinate them without corporate patent-holders' explicit permission. Even studying these plants can have legal consequences—if a science wants to research a lab-designed strain of wheat, their results become the property of the company that owns the wheat. This trend has sent biologists flocking to odd corners of the world in search of unpatented food crops they can examine . . . and has made the people in those parts of the world less than eager to hand over their grains for genetic sequencing.

This legal intolerance for ancient agricultural tradition is hardly the only example of a strange rigidity that permeates Western thinking about food. As soon as we ape-descended primitives began to have some choices as to what we would or wouldn't eat, we also began to be insanely judgmental about what other people chose to ingest.

Religious dietary laws, restrictive nutritional regimes and zero tolerance rules for alcohol all have their place. They can be sane and useful tools for promoting physical, mental and sometimes even societal well-being. Yet it is easy to go too far. Every diet has its overzealous devotees, those who will happily tell others that if they eat meat (or white sugar, or carbs, or fat), they will die. Somehow these nutritional preachers have managed to forget that life is fatal. That there is, as yet, no diet plan that confers immortality.

At the heart of all this societal confusion and mixed messages regarding food, though, the basics remain: eat and you live, starve and you die.

This simple reality is one that is often neglected in science fiction. Not entirely, of course: there are books like Mary Doria Russell's *The Sparrow*, in which human space explorers sample offworlder foods with sometimes-fatal results, even as they completely fail to notice where the alien race they've befriended gets its meat. There's Maureen McHugh's *Mission Child*, in which the soil of a new world colonized by humans has to be baked until every organic thing in it is dead, just so it can be laced with human-friendly microbes and nutrients.

But for every book that thoughtfully considers the nutritional underpinnings of human life, there are twenty in which food is a nonissue. Earth people eat alien food, aliens eat human food. Nobody gets sick and often—even during a crisis—nobody goes hungry.

In Hitchhiker's, by contrast, almost everyone needs to eat something, whether it's a Babel fish absorbing telepathic brainwaves, an ape-descended life-form like Arthur and Trillian, or an alien like Ford or Zaphod. It is no accident that the unhappiest character in this series of books is the one who literally cannot take comfort in food: Marvin, the Paranoid Android.

But why does it matter? Once you are beyond the point of chasing buffalo over cliffs just to work off the munchies, once you're well-off enough to get your calories in a cheesecake or a corn dog, once everything you eat comes wrapped in plastic and inspected by the government, you might think food would become a nonissue.

Not so. Arthur's experiences remind us that food fulfills needs that go far beyond mere survival. Having enough to eat is a biological necessity, but having *good* food is a pleasure few can resist. There's nothing like a hot, well-prepared meal. If it comes with good wine, a little ambiance, cushy chairs and someone else to wash the dishes and bring in the tiramisu after the main course, so much the better.

Little wonder, then, that food has played such a quiet but crucial role in great events throughout history. Europe's need for reliable spice routes spurred a wave of global exploration through the thirteenth to fifteenth centuries. A shortage of potatoes in Ireland led to widespread immigration to North America, while triggering land reform at home. A tax on sugar helped spark the American Revolution, while rising bread prices toppled the crown of France in 1789. Think about it: wars have been fought over groceries—and as often as not, the better-fed army is the one that wins.

Nowadays most of us in the wealthier nations don't worry about getting killed in a food riot, but that doesn't mean our food is risk free. Instead, the dangers of eating have become harder to weigh. Even if one rejects the idea that wheat or dairy products or chocolate are poisonous in their own right, there is no doubt that some foods can kill. The most notorious killer food is probably fugu, a form of blowfish that, unless prepared correctly, can poison an innocent diner in seconds. For those of us less prone to devouring exotic and potentially lethal delicacies, though, there remain eating-related hazards to consider. Will this steak give me BSE?, we can legitimately wonder; did I cook this hamburger enough to kill any E. coli bacteria that may have hitched a ride from the slaughterhouse to my kitchen counter? Is my fish contaminated with mercury? Will the pesticides in my fruit give me cancer?

More recently, we've also had to wonder: is this food genetically modified?

Back when Douglas Adams first wrote *The Hitchhiker's Guide to the Galaxy*, the idea of transgenic foods was the stuff of... well, of science fiction. It was 1994 when the U.S. Food and Drug Administration first approved the Flavr Savr tomato as safe and edible. In creating the Dish of the Day in *The Restaurant at the End of the Universe*, Adams wasn't commenting on an identifiable societal trend: he was foreseeing it.

Adams' vision was scary in its accuracy. The Dish of the Day is a genetically modified meat source as well as another trigger for Arthur's food-themed distress. Adams was so spot-on in his extrapolation that Arthur reacts to the Dish in much the same way we twenty-first-millennium froods have reacted to transgenic foods—first he is suspicious and then he refuses to eat it at all. (Note that not all humans are created equal—Trillian, who is in a far less threatened state of mind, digs in with a shrug.)

Trying to envision the future is one of the great pleasures of being an sf writer, and predicting something as accurately as Adams did GM foods is quite the coup. But *The Restaurant at the End of the Universe* isn't just about suicidal meat animals who talk. Back in the eighties, Adams had bigger fish to fry—the failure of big capitalism to deliver on its promises, the differences between elected leaders and the people who really wield power in so-called democracies, the pointless rush of developers to knock down perfectly good houses, or planets as the case may be, to create useless bypasses, and—most of all—homelessness.

Yes, homelessness. Another knee-slapper of a topic that Adams somehow managed to slip into his upbeat comic series.

Ever since humans came down from the trees, there have been people too poor to afford adequate shelter. In the eighties these numbers surged in Western democracies as a result of government cutbacks to affordable housing programs and other forms of social assistance. "Homelessness" became a household word, but it wasn't a new phenomenon. The so-called hobo of the thirties had become the bag lady of the eighties, who in turn has done a slow morph into the panhandler and squeegee kid of the present day. Despite our vast collective wealth and good intentions, the homeless have remained on our streets, apparently beyond our help.

What does this have to do with Arthur Dent?

When we readers first meet Arthur in *The Hitchhiker's Guide to the Galaxy*, he's on the verge of becoming homeless. The only way he's found to possibly avert that disastrous outcome is to lie in mud in front of a bulldozer, but it doesn't work. An hour later, his house is in ruins that are only slightly harder to see because the ruins, the bulldozers that made them and the entire planet have all been reduced to an even larger amount of rubble by the inappropriately named Vogon Constructor Fleet.

Arthur, in other words, is the ultimate homeless person.

When you're living on the rough, day-to-day existence becomes a fight for the essentials of survival. Finding a safe haven—preferably one whose captain isn't a Vogon bent on reading you poetry and tossing you into space—becomes paramount.

After safety from attack, of course, the only thing that matters more than finding shelter is finding food. But Arthur doesn't just want a full belly at any cost. That's about staying alive, but on some level he wants to savor life, if only for a moment. And so, what Arthur wants more than anything is a substance of limited nutritional value.

He wants tea.

Hot, comforting cups of tea are in short supply when the planet tea's grown on has boiled away into nothingness. That is precisely why Arthur wants one so badly. Cornflakes, sushi, anything grown on the Earth he has so recently lost would help, but it is tea he particularly wants, with all its soothing psychological connotations of British cultural superiority. Food is a necessity, tea a luxury. Nothing says you're all right quite as positively as a hot steaming cup of Darjeeling, served in bone china, if possible, with full-fat cream and silver spoons for the sugar. Tea implies safety and security, possession of spoons and creamers, a fire to drink by, a warm feather bed to lie down in.

Unfortunately for the perennially jumpy Arthur's nerves, tea is also caffeinated.

Luckily for Ford, Zaphod and Arthur's other exotic new friends, the whole tea hang-up seems to be very Earth-based. The comfort substance for the rest of them is much less likely to overstimulate the senses: alcohol.

Alcohol. Muscle relaxant. Destroyer of inhibitions. Ford and Zaphod know exactly where to find liquid comfort when the chips are down, and that's inside a nice deep gin bottle. When the Earth is about to meet its end, Ford collects Arthur and makes straight for the nearest pub. Zaphod, once his life's mission is complete, goes on an epic bender. Tea, gin, Pan Galactic Gargle Blaster—each character drinks to alleviate psychological anguish.

Really, with all the death and destruction of property in these books, it's a miracle Adams managed to make them funny. But really, at the heart of every truly great work of comedy is a droplet of immeasurable sadness. Hilarious though it may be, the Hitchhiker's trilogy draws much of its power from the sheer horror of Arthur's situation. Earth is gone and none of his attempts to recover it fully succeed. When he gets back to prehistoric times, he's faced with years of living in a cave, reduced to eating whatever he can catch. By the time he gets back to the substitute Earth provided by the dolphins, he no longer belongs there.

In another great English trilogy some of you may have heard of, J. R. R. Tolkien puts a quartet of hobbits through absolute hell. They are driven from their home, chased, assaulted and terrorized. Like Arthur, they sometimes reach temporary safe harbors . . . and the first thing their hosts do—whether Elvish, Entish or Gondorian—is lay out the food. They pile it high on the tables, get some extra-tall chairs and stuff those hobbits' bellies until they can't take any more. Then they tuck them into nice warm beds so they can sleep it off, all with the promise of an ample breakfast when they awake.

Arthur Dent should have it so good.

In *The Hitchhiker's Guide to the Galaxy*, he makes it to Magrathea. There is, indeed, a banquet laid. Ford, Zaphod and Trillian get to eat, just as they will in the Restaurant later. Before Arthur can sit down and tuck in, though, his mousey hosts Benjy and Franki announce that they want to purchase, remove and dice his brain. He is cheated of another meal when he finds himself unable to cope with the bioengineered niceties of eating the Dish of the Day in Milliways. Even his meal aboard the *Starship Bistromath* is full of uncertainty and arguments about the bill.

By the time Arthur makes it back to the replacement Earth in *So Long, and Thanks for All the Fish*, he has lost the capacity for hope or joy. Life could be good again, but it hasn't occurred to him to try to savor it. How do we know this? Because he gets back to his apartment and resignedly bolts down the three least toxic-looking items in his fridge, without regard to their taste or relative safety.

Slowly, however, Arthur's zest for life comes back. He starts small, by going to a bar, and eventually hooks up romantically with Fenchurch. Later, when he and Fenchurch finally make it to a good restaurant, he is utterly stunned by the experience of a good meal. He demands his waiter provide an explanation for it...and Fenchurch apologizes by explaining that Arthur is happy. It is at this moment that we readers realize that our hero's capacity for contentment has been renewed.

This is an entirely good thing, since Fenchurch disappears soon afterward.

But Arthur, we see, is still fine. He settles into the sandwich-making lifestyle on Bartledan and finds himself quite contented with it. He may not have a partner, but he is lacking for nothing else: he has a home, a remarkably prestigious job, a niche in the society of his adopted world. More than that, he takes pride in his profession, even working with his community to perfect sandwich knife designs. He's connected—he's gone from being uncomfortable even with himself to someone who fits in.

Now that Arthur is making food for others, he is revered for it, seen by the people of his newly adopted home village as a gift from their deity, Bob.

With his physical and psychological needs amply taken care of, Arthur throws himself wholeheartedly into bestowing food upon his neighbors. He has moved beyond awareness of his own suffering. When the end of *Mostly Harmless* comes—in a nightclub, as previously mentioned—he is at peace.

Like any hero of fiction, then, Arthur's journey becomes a mirror of our own. Most of us may have a fairly low chance of getting dragged across the cosmos in a ship powered by improbability. But we are all born helpless, with a single skill at birth—the ability to draw in nutrition and swallow. We move forward through time, encountering a host of things at least as odd as Ford Prefect, and if food cannot keep us alive forever, we certainly learn that the lack of it will surely kill. And we can all hope to be lucky enough to reach the same point as Arthur Dent before life's end: with everything we need readily to hand, an abundance of all the things that nourish not only the body but the spirit too, and a willingness to share those riches with others.

Now, with that in mind, perhaps it's time we all went and found ourselves a really good snack.

A resident of Vancouver, British Columbia, A. M. Dellamonica has been publishing science fiction and fantasy stories since the early nineties. Her next appearance in print will be an alternate history of Joan of Arc called "A Key to the Illuminated Heretic," due out in the anthology *Alternate Generals II* in spring 2005. Four of her works can be found anytime at SCIFI.COM, and her 2002 *Asimov's* piece, "A Slow Day at the Gallery," is out in *The Year's Best SF #8*. She writes book reviews for a number of magazines including *Science Fiction Weekly* (www.scifi.com/sfw) and maintains a Web site at http://www.sff.net/people/alyx.

Marguerite Krause

The Only Sane Man in the Universe

As the saying has it, "In the land of the blind, the one-eyed man would be king." This of course is nonsense. In the land of the blind, the one-eyed man would soon be burned as a witch or drawn and quartered for consorting with demons.

In the land of the insane, the sane man is a threat to society. Or, at least, very irritating. The voice of sanity, it turns out, is rarely one we want to hear.

ANALYZING HUMOR IS A DANGEROUS BUSINESS. Have you ever told a joke to a friend, been met with a blank stare, then tried to explain what was supposed to be funny about it? Your explanation probably didn't make your friend laugh, and might have permanently ruined the joke for you in the process. Humor that needs to be studied or translated in order to be appreciated likely wasn't all that funny to begin with.

That's part of the enduring pleasure of the Hitchhiker's Guide to the Galaxy. Its humor needs no explanation. Hitchhiker's Guide is a peculiar creation in any of its incarnations—radio program, book or TV series—full of odd characters dealing with bizarre events, written in a distinct, some would say utterly unique, style. But its best, funniest moments have a universal appeal, thanks in large part to the series' Everyman character, the indomitable Arthur Dent.

How can something unique have a universal appeal? And what's so special about Arthur Dent?

It's hardly unusual to have an Everyman character in a work of fiction. Writers have been putting them to good use for centuries. The Everyman or, in modern terms, the "audience identification" character, may serve as a vehicle for expressing the author's point of view or as a familiar touchstone for the reader (or listener or viewer) entering an unfamiliar universe—especially handy to have around in the literally out-of-this-world situations common to fantasy and science fiction stories. Arthur certainly serves both of those classic purposes. In addition, he is a particular kind of Everyman character: the "Only Sane Man in the Room"—or, given the scope of Hitchhiker's Guide, the Only Sane Man in the Universe.

In the classic Only Sane Man story, a preposterous situation exists which, for various reasons, is either ignored or accepted as normal by most of the characters. It's up to the OSM to, first, notice that the absurdity exists and then, in some cases, try to do something about it.

Although there are numerous variations on the OSM character, he is often an innocent of one kind or another, perhaps inexperienced, perhaps an outsider, pointing out the foibles of human nature or human society. One excellent example is the little child in Hans Christian Andersen's 1837 tale "The Emperor's New Clothes" who dares to defy authority and his culture's established norms of polite behavior to shout "The emperor is naked!" for everyone to hear. That wise little child exhibits another common trait of OSM characters: apparent powerlessness. The OSM sees more clearly—more sanely—that anyone else, but for various reasons lacks the ability to make the changes that would set an off-kilter situation right.

This, of course, is exactly the sort of irresolvable conflict that makes for entertaining comedy. The one person who is able to recognize a problem is also the one person who's not allowed to fix it. Humorous stories with an OSM character appeal to us for two main reasons. First, we've all known what it's like to be the only sane person in the room. Perhaps as a teen confronting an unreasonable parent, or an employee stuck with an impossible boss, we know the frustration of feeling as if we were the sole sensible person in a senseless world. Second, depending on how the OSM deals with his particular troubles, we either take vicarious pleasure in his triumph or watch his downfall with a combination of sympathetic horror and the supreme confidence that, faced with the same circumstances, we would do better.

What makes Arthur Dent such a memorable OSM is the distinct style with which he faces all the adversity that Douglas Adams throws at him. But, as unique as Arthur is, he didn't spring into existence out of thin air. Douglas Adams was a talented writer in a long line of clever British humorists, and the influence of his predecessors and contemporaries can be found throughout Hitchhiker's Guide. It's fun to identify a few of those common themes and techniques—and even more fascinating to see how Arthur differs from other OSM characters that came before him or have followed after.

Any discussion of British humor has to include the author P. G. Wodehouse. Born in Guildford in 1881, Wodehouse wrote short stories for magazines, lyrics for musical comedies and over ninety novels, sharing his intelligent, wry, often just plain silly sense of humor with generations of fans—including Douglas Adams. If you pick up any of Wodehouse's books and leaf through the pages, readers familiar with Hitchhiker's Guide are likely to feel immediately at home.

For example, here is a typical Wodehousian turn of phrase:

...a totally new experience, causing him to wonder what had hit him—like a man who, stooping to pluck a nosegay of wild flowers on a railway line, is unexpectedly struck in the small of the back by the Cornish Express. (*Jeeves in the Morning,* 1971)

That's a clever comedic effect—set up a familiar situation, then give it an unexpected twist—but not unique. A better example of the influence

Wodehouse had on Adams is a passage like this one, in which a man is worrying about his fiancée's low opinion of his financial situation:

> ...Claire saw to it that these doubts sprouted, by confining her conversation on the occasions of their meeting almost entirely to the great theme of money, with its minor sub-divisions of How to get it, Why don't you get it? and I'm sick and tired of not having it. (*Uneasy Money*, 1917)

Sound familiar? Compare the flow and rhythm with:

> The History of every major Galactic Civilization tends to pass through three distinct and recognizable phases...the first phase is characterized by the question, "How can we eat?" the second by the question, "Why do we eat?" and the third by the question, "Where shall we have lunch?" (*The Restaurant at the End of the Universe*, 1980)

Or, even better:

> ...a book called *The Hitchhiker's Guide to the Galaxy*...more controversial than Oolon Colluphid's trilogy of philosophical blockbusters *Where God Went Wrong, Some More of God's Greatest Mistakes* and *Who is this God Person Anyway?* (*The Hitchhiker's Guide to the Galaxy*, 1979)

In addition to Wodehouse, two other likely influences on Adams' sense of humor deserve mention. *The Goon Show,* a radio comedy and music program in the 1950s written and performed by Spike Milligan, Peter Sellers and Harry Secombe, is an obvious candidate for the role of dotty grandfather to Hitchhiker's Guide. A comedy sketch on *The Goon Show* often began with an Everyman trying to cope with an ordinary situation run amok. For instance, in the episode "Wings Over Dagenham" (first aired January 1957), an army unit is running low on supplies, so Everyman Ned and his dim-witted companion Eccles have to, among other things, invent the airplane, discover the existence of the British Air Ministry and learn to fly before they can relieve the beleaguered soldiers.

By modern standards, however, and especially compared with Hitchhiker's Guide, *Goon Show* humor is gentle in content and quaintly self-conscious in tone. In the recordings of the programs, you can hear the cast members laughing right along with the studio audience, delighted by their own wit. Some of the strange characters and character voices provided by Peter Sellers remain as amusingly bizarre as when they were first created. But for the most part, although the comedy was cleverly innovative for its time, today it's mostly just silly, and the punch lines predictable. For instance, when Ned, after inventing the airplane, is trying to get permission to take off from an uncooperative Air Minister, Ned gets so frustrated that he begins to sputter in wordless indignation, to which the Air Minister replies: "I see you're a wit as well." Hardly a brilliant remark these days, but the 1950s audience howled with laughter.

Here's one more example of classic *Goon Show* humor, again from the "Wings Over Dagenham" episode. One of the objectives of their mission, in addition to delivering supplies, is to determine whether the Earth is flat or spherical. Once they're airborne, Ned and Eccles have the following conversation:

ECCLES: I just saw the Earth through the clouds.
NED: Did it look round?
ECCLES: Yeah, but I didn't think it saw me.

To our ears today, *Goon Show* humor has more in common with vaudeville, or nightclub stand-up comedy of the 1950s and 1960s, than with Douglas Adams' work on Hitchiker's Guide.

A more obvious antecedent to Hitchiker's Guide is the television sketch comedy of Monty Python's Flying Circus, first written and performed just a few years before Douglas Adams created Hitchiker's Guide—which makes Monty Python not so much an ancestor as a sibling. Countless Monty Python sketches start from the same foundation as Hitchiker's Guide: a British Everyman, minding his own business, encounters an utterly absurd situation and soon realizes that he is the Only Sane Man in the Room.

Precisely how does an OSM character react when faced with life's adversities? There seems to be a tried-and-true three-stage process:

1. Get a clear understanding of the situation
2. Explain the problem, as you see it, to the people around you, especially if you think they're in a position to fix it
3. If reasonable persuasion fails, attack the problem yourself with the OSM's weapon of choice: withering sarcasm

A perfect example of the OSM approach to life is Monty Python's "The Dead Parrot Sketch." John Cleese plays a customer returning a dead Norwegian Blue parrot to a pet shop. In step one, the customer proclaims his firm grasp of the situation: the parrot is dead. The clerk (Michael Palin) tries to dismiss him, saying of the stiff, motionless bird, "It's resting," and, "It's pining for the fjords." In step two, the customer insists on the facts ("It's stone dead") and complains that the only reason the bird was upright to begin with was that the clerk had nailed it to the perch. The clerk says he did that because otherwise it would have muscled its way out of the cage: "Vroom!" To this, the customer replies, "This parrot wouldn't vroom if you put 4,000 volts through it. If you hadn't nailed it to the perch it would be pushing up the daisies," and continues his eloquent step three with a lengthy list of synonyms and euphemisms for "dead" until, at last, the clerk surrenders and agrees to replace the bird.

Writers working in a longer format than a three-minute sketch—such as novels or a multi-episode radio program—can develop the OSM's three-stage reaction to life's absurdities at a more leisurely pace.

For example: step one, identify the problem:

"Where's Dawlish?" he said.
"He has gone."
"Gone? How do you mean—gone? You don't mean—gone?"
"Yes."
"Gone away?"
"Gone away."
"You don't mean—gone away?"
"Yes."
"Do you mean—gone away?"
"Yes." (*Uneasy Money* by P. G. Wodehouse, 1917)

FORD: How would you react if I told you that I'm not from Guildford after all, but from a small planet somewhere in the vicinity of Betelgeuse?

ARTHUR: I don't know. Why? Do you think it's the sort of thing you're likely to say? (*The Hitchiker's Guide to the Galaxy* radio program, episode 1, 1977)

Step two: once you understand what's going on, explain the situation to everyone around you. Many people would agree that one of Arthur's most distinctive and defining traits as the Only Sane Man in the Universe is his dedication to stating the obvious as many times as necessary to get his point across:

> FORD (in the Vogon airlock):...and we'll shoot out into deep space and asphyxiate in about thirty seconds.
> ARTHUR: So this is it — we're going to die! (*The Hitchiker's Guide to the Galaxy* radio program, episode 2, 1977)

> "Hey, this is terrific! Someone down there is trying to kill us!"
> "Terrific," said Arthur.
> "But don't you see what this means?"
> "Yes. We're going to die." (*The Hitchhiker's Guide to the Galaxy*, 1979)

> EDDIE: Impact minus fifteen seconds, guys.
> ARTHUR: The missiles are still homing in. You can't shake them. We're going to die!
> (And shortly thereafter:)
> ARTHUR: It's no good. The missiles are swinging around after us and gaining fast. We are quite definitely going to die! (*The Hitchiker's Guide to the Galaxy* radio program, episode 2, 1977)

Finally, step three: the Only Sane Man in the Universe, unable to convince anyone else of the seriousness of the situation, resorts to attacking the problem with sarcasm. In a dictionary, sarcasm might be defined as "a mocking remark using statements opposite or irrelevant to the underlying intent." In everyday life, sarcasm has probably been around for as long as people have been asking foolish questions:

> CRO-MAGNON ONE: Oops! I just dropped that rock on your foot. Does it hurt?
> CRO-MAGNON TWO: No, of course not. All this hopping around and yelling is part of a new fertility dance I've been working on....

Sarcasm is more than just witty humor. It can be used to aggressively attack an opponent, or as a form of self-defense (or self-delusion): if you keep busy making witty, disparaging remarks you won't have time to deal with how miserably terrified you are. Telling the difference between various levels and purposes of sarcasm often comes down to recognizing the speaker's tone of voice. That's one reason why sarcasm written for radio, television or film acquires whole new levels of intensity and nuance from the actor who performs the lines.

British writers don't have a monopoly on sarcasm, of course:

KERMIT (in a restaurant, to waiter): You may serve us now.

WAITER: Oh, may I?

In that scene from *The Muppet Movie* (1979), the waiter was played by Steve Martin, a master of American sarcastic delivery. It's an example of a straightforward, no-nonsense sort of sarcasm, performed and perfected for years by stand-up comics like Martin, Lenny Bruce, Dick Gregory and the legendary inventor of "insult comedy," Don Rickles: pure, unashamed aggression disguised as entertainment, making it socially acceptable to express contempt and rage. That kind of biting, anger-driven sarcasm provides a great vehicle for criticizing powerful individuals or organizations. It's the Rebel defying Authority, the Little Guy standing up to the Bully—American mythology played out with verbal violence instead of guns.

OSM characters in British humorous fiction also sometimes use sarcasm to protest societal injustice. The pet store customer in "The Dead Parrot Sketch" is one example; another is Arthur, objecting to the council's decision to demolish his house. At other times, though, the OSM is just trying to find a way to make it through his own absurdly lousy day. For instance, in the film *Galaxy Quest* (1999), a group of actors who once were stars of a popular science fiction television show find themselves having to reenact their roles on a real spaceship in a battle with real evil aliens. Each of them responds to this impossible situation with varying levels of shock, disbelief, terror or delight. In this predominantly American film, the Only Sane Man in the Room turns out to be Alex, performed with sardonic flair by British actor Alan Rickman. When Tommy, the helmsman, tries to pilot the ship through a minefield and keeps running into and exploding the mines, it is Alex who shouts, in classic, distraught OSM fashion, "Could you possibly try not to hit every single one?"

John Cleese, the Monty Python veteran, wrote and performed one of the most eloquent—and most ultimately hopeless—OSM characters ever for the television series *Fawlty Towers*. Basil Fawlty (Cleese), who runs a hotel with his wife, Sybil, considers himself the Only Sane Man in the Room, and is constantly protesting what he sees as the injustice and absurdity of his existence. In reality, Fawlty himself is usually to blame for the chaos in his life, but he devotes so much time and energy to attacking his foes with his rapier wit that he never recognizes his own contribution to the problem.

For instance, in the 1979 episode "Basil the Rat," Fawlty walks into the hotel kitchen to find a stranger poking around in the refrigerator. Rather than simply ask the man what he's doing—and thereby learn that he's the health inspector—Fawlty launches into a sarcastic attack, beginning with, "Shall I get you the wine list?" and concluding, when Sybil enters, with "May I introduce the gentleman who's just opened the self-service department here?" Too often, Fawlty's attempts to fight life's "absurdities" with wit backfire; instead of correcting a bad situation, he makes a harmless situation bad.

Sometimes, though, we can't help agreeing with Fawlty's response to life's frustrations, as in this exchange:

> DIFFICULT GUEST (looking out her hotel room window): When I pay for a view, I expect something more interesting than that.
>
> FAWLTY: That's Torquay, madam.
>
> DIFFICULT GUEST: Well, it's not good enough.
>
> FAWLTY: Well, may I ask what you were expecting to see out of a Torquay hotel bedroom window? Sydney Opera House, perhaps? The Hanging Gardens of Babylon? Herds of wildebeests sweeping majestically....
>
> DIFFICULT GUEST: Don't be silly.... (*Fawlty Towers*, "Communications Problems," 1979)

A few things make Arthur unique among OSM characters in humorous fiction. One is that Arthur's problems are larger than vain friends, obnoxious hotel customers or the need to return a dead parrot to a pet shop. As a result, he spends much of the story—quite reasonably, one could argue—teetering on the brink of hysteria. The only thing that keeps him from collapsing in a corner in a gibbering panic with his towel draped over his head is his conviction that he is the Only Sane Man in the Universe and therefore has a responsibility to try to make sense of everything that happens to him. Again and again, like any OSM, Arthur follows the classic three-step strategy. He struggles to understand absurd events, suggests logical solutions to problems and then, when being reasonable doesn't work, he attacks with sarcasm. However, maybe because of the sheer scope of his problems, Arthur rises to unparalleled heights of OSM eloquence. Two perfect examples of Arthur's distinctive style occur near the beginning of his adventures. When Arthur learns that the city council intends to demolish his house, the city representative, Mr. Prosser, insists that Arthur should have lodged a complaint when the plans were first announced to the public:

> "But look, you found the notice didn't you?"
> "Yes," said Arthur, "yes I did. It was on display in the bottom of a locked filing cabinet stuck in a disused lavatory with a sign on the door saying *Beware of the Leopard*." (*The Hitchhiker's Guide to the Galaxy*, 1979)

And a short while later, right after the Earth is destroyed:

FORD: We're safe.
ARTHUR: Oh, good.
FORD: We're in a small galley cabin in one of the spaceships of the Vogon Constructor Fleet.
ARTHUR: Ah, this is obviously some strange usage of the word "safe" that I wasn't previously aware of. (*The Hitchhiker's Guide to the Galaxy* television series, episode 1, 1980)

The final detail that makes Arthur unique among OSM characters is his ultimate fate. In some stories, such as "The Emperor's New Clothes" or "The Dead Parrot Sketch," the OSM's voice of reason persuades the people around him to accept his viewpoint and save the world. In other stories, such as *Fawlty Towers*, although the OSM is powerless to change his circumstances, he never loses his conviction that they need to be changed. Knowing that he is right and everyone else is crazy, the helpless OSM keeps on protesting the world's insanity on the off chance that someone, sometime, will heed his warnings and set things right.

Arthur follows a different path. As the story of Hitchhiker's Guide progresses—especially if you follow it through the initial four books—Arthur's confidence that he is the Only Sane Man in the Universe falters. Eventually, he abandons the notion altogether. Starting on the day the Vogons arrive, events conspire to turn Arthur's worldview upside down. In the beginning, like any OSM character, Arthur believes that the universe is a rational place. He imagines that he has a reasonable grasp of how life is supposed to work and that it's his job to point out any temporary flaws or inconsistencies that may be disrupting the natural order.

The problem is that there *is* no underlying sense or sanity in Douglas Adams' worldview. Arthur is the Only Sane Man in an *insane* universe. That's why all of his rational analyses and righteous outrage consistently fail to help him cope with the situations he finds himself in.

On the bright side, this means that Arthur's frequent insistence that "We are quite definitely going to die!" always turns out to be wrong. Still, it takes him a long time—well into *So Long, andThanks for All the Fish*—to learn that being the OSM is not only unnecessary, it's doing him more harm than good. Gradually, his experiences force him to give up all three steps of OSM behavior: the sarcasm, the attempts to convince other people to see things his way and even the basic belief that it's humanly possible to understand anything. We see this resignation in his response to Fenchurch, who is trying to describe what she remembers about the day the Earth was destroyed:

> "Arthur, I mean this, this is very real to me, this is serious."
> "*I* was being perfectly serious," said Arthur; "it's just the Universe I'm never quite sure about." (*So Long, and Thanks for All the Fish*, 1984)

As a comedic character, Arthur is at his funniest when he is playing the role of Only Sane Man in the Universe. But as the story progresses, Arthur evolves. He recognizes the wisdom of the advice he received during his visit to Magrathea:

> SLARTIBARTFAST (on the subject of figuring out the meaning of life): I always think the chances of finding out what really is going on are so absurdly remote that the only thing to do is to say hang the sense of it and just keep yourself occupied. (*The Hitchiker's Guide to the Galaxy* television series, episode 4, 1980)

This might be the core message of Hitchhiker's Guide: If the universe itself is a joke, there's no point in trying to deal reasonably with it. Like many of us, Arthur sees things that are wrong in the world and desperately wants to fix them. Unlike similar humorous fictional characters, though, Arthur grows beyond his original role in the story and eventually expresses a viewpoint that's the complete reverse of the one he started with. Instead of demanding that the universe fit his expectations for logic and order, he learns to accept the universality of disorder and thrive on the unexpected and the nonsensical.

What makes Arthur such a simultaneously universal and unique character is that only by giving up his most basic convictions does he succeed, on a personal level, in finding true happiness.

And that, for Arthur, is the ultimate meaning of Life, the Universe and Everything.

Marguerite Krause's favorite activities involve the printed word. In addition to writing, she works as a freelance copy editor, helping other writers to sharpen their skills, and for relaxation loves nothing better than to curl up with a good book. She is married to her high school sweetheart; they have two children. You can find more of Marguerite's writing in the anthologies *Seven Seasons of* Buffy and *Five Seasons of* Angel; her two-part epic fantasy, *Moons' Dreaming* and *Moons' Dancing*, co-written with Susan Sizemore; and her fantasy novel, *Blind Vision*.

John Shirley

Douglas Adams
and the Wisdom
of Madness

Two decades ago a wise and sane man reached an important conclusion. "It seems to me," he decided, "that any civilization that had so far lost its head as to need to include a set of detailed instructions for use in a package of toothpicks, was no longer a civilization in which I could live and stay sane."

That was twenty years ago. It's gotten worse since then. Much much worse.

"...the howl of clashing colors, the intertwining of all contradictions, grotesqueries, trivialities: LIFE."
—TRISTAN TZARA

MISFITS MAY HAVE AN EDGE. I've had that advantageous disadvantage. Born baseline spacey and intellectually restless, traumatized by a neighbor at seven, my father dying when I was ten, moving six times before I was twelve, and confirming, when I moved to a new place, that people everywhere are oriented to pecking orders; that many of them are hostile to those who are different; that children who should be friendly and playful are often violent and cruel—look for my picture in the dictionary under *misfit*.

Being a misfit, I saw that what we're taught about the world—that schools are "fair," that the law is "fair," that people are usually friendly to strangers—was contradicted by reality at its most basic. I recognized the contradictions in life and absorbed the dire facts about human nature sooner than most people do. The absurdities and inequities come home to the misfit sooner—it's that pecking order thing. It makes sure you get it. Hence the misfit may have a bit of an edge in terms of appreciating the quandary of the human condition. The misfit will be a little less likely to be shattered, perhaps, when the center doesn't hold, and things fall apart, because it's always been off center and breaking down, for him. For her.

In the 1980s I became a punk-rock singer as a way to adapt to the apparent hostility of life; later, when I wrote and published outlandish science fiction and horror novels, it was really a kind of protest poetry about life's intimidating vastness and bizarrity, its offhanded dismissal of human priorities…

The tendency to adapt to life's contradictions this way, while giving me a misfit's edge, might also cultivate a certain permeability between me and the world of my own imagination.

As for example…

Just the other day, I had a conversation with an imaginary alien from another world. I said imaginary—I didn't say he didn't exist. He's been "a part of me" since I missed an important catch in a softball game, at the age of eight. I'd been staring up at the sky, thinking about planets, when I saw a white sphere coming toward me, ever so slowly and gracefully. Here, in person, was one of the spheres of heaven! I watched in fascination as it came closer and closer—dimly aware of people somewhere yelling at me to do something. It fell right in front of me and rolled, coming to a stop against my toe. Only then did I realize it was a softball.

Having added to the losing team's miseries, I was cornered by certain players, afterward, and smacked about, as the coach smilingly looked the other way. At that point the imaginary alien in me was born. (Perhaps my contemplation of celestial spheres had summoned him from one of them.)

The alien, however, now claims to be leaving our world (I doubt he can, so long as I'm here, but never mind), out of sheer disgust with our lunacy.

Sounds "kind of Douglas Adams," doesn't it? The human condition is absurd, is insane, laughable even when it's tragic—that's the feeling you get from the novels of the late Douglas Adams.

But if you really think about it, this alien being's point of view on us is somewhat distinct from Adams'. The brilliant author of The Hitchhiker's Guide to the Galaxy series, so far as I can tell, sees *all* existence as quite mad—not just our world. But this alien is in denial about the extent of the madness. He may be right that it is in many ways worse here, on Earth—and of course Adams, who was (ostensibly) a native of the planet Earth, may have had his view of the universe skewed by his planetary origins.

I have transcribed most of my recent conversation with the alien from another world (I am leaving out the parts where he complains about Paris Hilton, giant parking lots and casinos, and reality television). Although he may be an imaginary alien engaged in an imaginary conversation, the events he refers to are all quite real, I'm sorry to say. Here's the transcription:

So, alien from another world, I understand you're leaving our planet. Should we be relieved?

Yeah man, I was going to lead a takeover of the planet—but we're, like, totally *not interested* anymore. Enslave *you* people? We don't want to be anywhere *near* you. It's trash, dude. You people are profoundly messed up. I mean, yeah, we're ruthless invaders from another world, but we don't pay tens of thousands of dollars on eBay for a cheese sandwich with a lady's face on it, which truly recently happened on your benighted world—

One aside here, alien, your use of dialect, here, is like a human from our world, sort of colloquial Californian—what's up with that?

I'm an observer, I'm a linguist, I picked up the dialect, what do you want, I'm supposed to do a bad job? I'm a hella good linguist, dude. And where you are you from? California. If I was talking to certain Africans I'd be making clicking noises. Anyway, back to the cheese sandwich of God—for real, you people bid big financial resources on a toasted cheese sandwich on eBay because someone thought they saw a picture of the "Virgin Mary" on it. I remember when there was that tortilla with "Jesus" on it, in Mexico—*that* was ludicrous enough... but this! I mean—we were shocked that you people strap bombs on yourselves and blow yourselves up in the name of being Helpful; we were shocked by the rape camps in the Sudan—whoa, I thought *we* were ruthless— and we were shocked that you people in America insist, despite all the evidence, that you actually *elected* your newest president. But the toasted cheese sandwich, boys, for thousands of dollars on eBay? That's over the line... The whole Virgin Mary concept in the first place is, frankly, scientifically untenable. But the Virgin Mary *sandwich?*

You sure you even comprehend sandwiches, alien?

What? You think we don't have sandwiches on our planet? We put radioactive plankton between a couple of sheets of flying-dog-skin, not exactly your kind of sandwich, but it's still a sandwich—delicious, too, especially with a little sprinkle of hopping-squid neurons... Anyway, this sandwich of yours, it's going on tour, did you know that? Pilgrims are going to line up to see it.

Still, we're better off being what we are than being enslaved by you, aren't we?

You'd be better off than running things yourselves. Let me give you some examples, all taken from a couple of ordinary newspapers. According to a newspaper survey, almost half of the people in your country believe the universe was created less than 70,000 years ago. This is in an era when you people are sending probes to other planets and learning to line up atoms with nanotechnology (that's something I learned one day in third grade, right before recess, on my world, but never mind.) Yet they believe that two naked people in a garden, after being snookered by a snake, started the human race. These believers are opposed to incest but they don't mind that they themselves are said to be the product of interbreeding between the children of these two proto humans. One of these Faithful, a pharmacist in Texas, recently refused to sell birth control because it "destroys lives." The male body creates more than 200 million sperm for every single ejaculation. Presumably when he ejaculates, the pharmacist catches all the extra run-off in a cup and saves the little fellas in jars, feeding them with microscopic tweezers.

That's not the only religion on this planet, alien, be fair—

Right you are, there are lots of others, mostly quite loony. Millions of Muslims quote the Hadith which says that "The least reward for the each of the people of Heaven is 80,000 servants and 72 virginal wives, over which stands a dome of pearls, aquamarine and ruby." A good many of these Muslims believe that you can get these rewards by stoning women to death, and killing thousands of innocent people with hijacked flying vehicles. Certain Muslims recently aired a French television special earnestly stating that the Jewish people created and disseminated the HIV virus. Meanwhile, in Libya, five nurses and a doctor from Palestine in *actual* fact used syringes to deliberately infect more than 400 children with HIV. But hey, not to be outdone, the Israeli Army recently shot down a ten-year-old Palestinian girl as she approached an Army post. At first this terrified kid was just wounded in the leg, but a conscientious Israeli officer walked up to her and emptied his gun into her, ten rounds at close range. He said he was "confirming the kill." Shall we talk about Rwanda? 800,000 Tutsi people, butchered by the Hutu, over ten days—and why? Because these Tutsis were problematic, being "a different tribe"—even though they shared the *same language* with the Hutus, had the *same history*, the *same cultural traditions*, often worked in the *same places*! But, you know, hey, they're *Tutsis*! Hack them to death with machetes!

Well, there are sick people on this planet but—

Sick people? On this planet? Oh *noooooo!* An orange, an eggplant, a flashlight bulb, a screw, a crayon, a pencil, a candle, part of a wooden shoe tree, a drinking glass—

What's this list?

A Coca-Cola bottle, a brandy bottle, carrots, a jade bracelet, avian pulmonary tissue, an oxidized iron rod, a dead parakeet—all things found by doctors stuck in women's vaginas. Now as to the objects found in the rectal cavities of—

That's okay, alien, thanks for sharing. Listen—the *average* person isn't so twisted...Joe American isn't insane...

No? Here, this is from the news around Thanksgiving: In West Virginia, Jackie Lee Shrader, 49, and his son, Harley Lee, 24, had a brief shootout with .22-caliber handguns when the pair confronted each other over how to cook skinless chicken for dinner. In Alaska, Niccolo Rossodivita, 62, shot Billy Cordova, 40, twice in the chest in an argument about Jesus Christ's correct name. In Eugene, Oregon, Angela Morris, 19, was charged with assaulting her boyfriend by pouring boiling oil on him during an argument over a Bible verse the two had been reading...Also over Thanksgiving this year, a guy in Massachusetts stabbed two members of his family for criticizing him for eating his turkey with his fingers.

I know it looks bad—

Come on, you really expect us to *invade* this psychotic planet? You people are sick! We want nothing more to do with you—not even invasion! See a damn doctor, or something. Six billion doctors. I'm leaving, I'm going to a planet where they juggle jellyfish to express their angst. Those people make *sense* compared to you Earth types.

You won't reconsider?

No—suppose you people somehow infect our world with those *Starbucks* things? No, dude, I'm outta here. 'Bye.

...And that's all he'd say.

My disgruntled alien has a point: this planet could be viewed as one enormous, badly maintained, poorly funded lunatic asylum. But is it our fault? The psychiatrist R.D. Laing argued that those of us who seem mentally ill are simply adapting to an insane world, to unbearable, maddening tensions set up by the world's contradictions, its inherent cognitive dissonances. Madness should be valued, Laing said, as a kind of longterm epiphanic experience, cathartic and strangely healthy.

It seems to me that's the theme we find in Douglas Adams, again and again. In life, as in the Adams canon, madness leads to madness which leads to more madness—and you adapt however you can. Usually with...a kind of madness.

However, let's be clear: there's unhealthy madness—and then there's a kind of *wise insanity*. Adams satirizes the first and by implication advocates the second.

A Catholic theologian recently pointed out that, according to the calculations of certain historians, in the entire history of the human race there have been *only 350 years without war*. That's a day here, a few weeks there, adding up. War is the human condition. Despite the apparent calm in much of America and Europe, you know, in your heart, that you could be swept up in war any time—post 9/11 you know it not only in your heart, but in your head.

You are expected to adapt to that knowledge, willy-nilly. But how? Usually with denial, as far as that'll take us—and the kind of madness that's made to *sound* rational: with the insane reasonable-sounding systems that Adams mocks so often in his work.

Your president tells you that he's going to end terrorism by invading another country, while at the same time he is frequently advised by pretty much everyone that invading that country will *foment* terrorism; when it *does* produce more terrorism, he beams and points to the "progress" made in ending terrorism. In effect he's saying, "Cultivating terrorism ends terrorism!"

Adapt to that.

(I adapted by seriously considering emigrating to Canada: surely a symptom of impending madness.)

You're minding your business, selling socks and Egyptian cigarettes in Baghdad, and some CIA bureaucrat's confused intel leads to your being chucked in the back of a humvee, taken to Abu Ghraib where, in the name of defending freedom, American soldiers make you play with yourself in front of your fellow Muslims, and then pile your body into a heap with other naked prisoners for a photo op.

Adapt to that.

(Some adapt by strapping bombs on themselves: insane violence as an adaptation. That's the *bad* adaptive-insanity I mentioned.)

The human mind is designed to find patterns, to consolidate chaos into order, to seek to harmonize contradictions. It works okay when you're figuring out how to build a boat to cross a river. But you mustn't look for big, overall patterns that really make sense of things as a whole—if you do, you get scared by how meaningless life can seem. That way lies madness.

Just try complaining about the situation. In the novel, *The Hitchhiker's Guide to the Galaxy,* we're told that the Complaints Division of the Sirius Cybernetics Corporation covers the major land masses of three medium-sized planets. The company has this motto: *Share and Enjoy.* When the three-mile-high sign displaying the motto collapses,[1] the damaged remains of the sign then appears to read, "Go stick your head in a pig."

This seems to suggest that the real motto of this gigantic, ubiquitous corporation *is* in fact "Go stick your head in a pig." Giant corporations, like bureaucracies and governments, are always revealed, in Adams, to be the Hell that is more than the sum of the parts. They are insistently

---

[1] The sign's collapse killed great numbers of Complaints executives—consistently, in Adams, thousands, even millions of people are seen to be casually exterminated by ruthless, random circumstance.

irrational, and strangely powerful in their irrationality. Their obstinate irrationality seems almost an asset to them, though it is a liability to you.

Even the Hitchhiker's Guide of the story, itself, issuing from the mega-sized Megadodo Publications (decode the name: Megadodo = Giant Stupidity), can be relied on to be unreliable, and arrogantly so. Adams says that it "does at least make the reassuring claim, that where it is inaccurate it is at least definitively inaccurate. In cases of major discrepancy it's always reality that got it wrong."

That's the fundamental social disconnect—something we find satirized in Jonathan Swift (whom Adams resembles, quite often), in Mark Twain (as for example his *A Yankee in King Arthur's Court*, and Adams has been compared to Sam Clemens too), in Monty Python (Adams had some connections to them), and very sharply in Adams' *The Restaurant at the End of the Universe*: The hapless Ford Prefect and the even more hapless Arthur Dent find themselves crash-landing on a mystery planet, where they're bunged in with the idiotic Golgafrinchans. Hundreds of thousands of Golgafrinchans, people from an advanced civilization, are stranded in a wilderness, without fire or the wheel, where they spend their time "giving grants," making committees for virtually everything, including working out how to start a fire. After five hundred and seventy three committee meetings, a former hairdresser given two pieces of wood for fire-starting research returns with his handiwork: the wood has been made into curling irons. The former hairdresser, stranded on an alien world, obstinately insists on continuing as a hairdresser exactly where hairdressers are least needed. When Ford criticizes their fire-making efforts, a Golgafrinchan girl responds:

> "Well, you're obviously being totally naïve of course...When you've been in marketing as long as I have you'll know that before any new product can be developed it has to be properly researched. We've got to find out what people want from fire, how they relate to it, what sort of image it has for them."

How about building the wheel, at least, Ford begs them.

> "Ah," said the marketing girl, "well, we're having a little difficulty there."
> "Difficulty?" exclaimed Ford. "Difficulty? What do you mean, difficulty? It's the single simplest machine in the entire universe!"
> The marketing girl soured him with a look.

"All right, Mr Wiseguy," she said, "you're so clever, you tell us what color it should be."

This ordinary madness, superimposing meaningless conceptual frameworks on irrelevant situations, realities that won't fit into the frames, is a fundamental human characteristic that Adams instinctively sends up whenever he can. (Vonnegut and Joseph Heller did it too, but not as farcically.) We demand the irrelevant. We're always stuck in some half-remembered model of the past, never really looking around at the now, never just taking it in for what it is.

We get scant direct philosophical input from Adams—nothing he doesn't contradict a moment later, usually. He seems to be *implying*, however, that uncertainty is the only certainty, and a kind of *enlightened uncertainty* can be an intelligent way to approach reality. Trillian and Zaphod Beeblebrox, and by extension Adams, approve when the whiskey-tippling old man thought to be the secret master of the cosmos replies, when asked if he believes in anything,

> "I don't know. I've never met all these people you speak of. And neither, I suspect, have you. They only exist in words we hear. It is folly to say you know what is happening to other people. Only they know, if they exist. They have their own Universes of their eyes and ears."

The old gent, living contentedly in a tin-roofed shack on a rainy planet with his scruffy cat, seems to embody a kind of infinite compassion as he refuses to judge anyone, or anything, understanding the subjectivity of the existential condition; he seems detached from identification, unwilling to engage in any set assumption about reality based merely on past experiences. "How can I tell," he asks, "that the past isn't a fiction designed to account for the discrepancy between my immediate physical sensations and the state of my mind."

Well, there it is, he's laying it out for us: The disconnect. The acknowledgement of the tendency to impose presumptions, prejudices, narrowings on a reality—ever-dynamic, evolving—that won't be imposed upon. The old man seems crazy—and yet he's the sanest one in the scene.

Zaphod approves:

> "I think the Universe is in pretty good hands, yeah?"
> "Very good," said Trillian. They walked off into the rain.

Now writers, I can attest, do sometimes "put themselves" into their own fiction but typically they are only inserting *sub*-selves, portions of their personalities, as if they're trying to see these temporary manifestations of themselves objectively; trying to see the various facets of themselves as they really are. A protagonist may represent one side of me, when I write a novel; an antagonist may represent another side of me.

Zaphod, mercurial and whimsical, may represent some part of Adams himself, as Arthur Dent, very British and ready to lie down in front of a bulldozer (Adams was a committed environmentalist) is another. Zaphod approves of the old man's philosophy: adapt to reality, remain skeptical, don't get caught up any one aspect of it so that you lose touch with the whole flow.

This also dovetails with Adams' remark, in *Restaurant,* to wit that people who most want to be rulers are "least suited to it." That could have been a remark by the Taoist philosopher Lao Tzu.

The Hitchhiker's Guide to the Galaxy (the novel) more or less starts with Arthur Dent learning that some confused bureaucracy has permitted that his house be razed, pets and all. Adams then takes it to a much higher level, when the diabolically dull and brutish Vogons demolish the entire Earth, in moments, to make room for an interstellar throughway ramp. In the second book of the series, we're told in a casual aside that a planet with millions of souls on it was used as a kind of giant pool ball, knocked into a black hole and destroyed for points in a game. In *Life, the Universe and Everything* the inhabitants of the planet Krikkit are planning the destruction of the cosmos merely because *they're sick of looking at it.*

The universe is violent, and unfair. Our human ideas of fairness, normalcy and sanity are based on tiny perceptions, and are quite futile. Look, about the time I figured out how to live life, I was well past forty—past the part where I could have used the knowledge to shape my life. This same profoundly annoying realization has come to hundreds of millions, probably billions of people: youth is wasted on the young. Life is inherently unfair, unjust—the only "justice," apart from the laws of physics, is what we create ourselves.

So far as anyone scientific can make out, the purpose of our brutish and short existence is to be carriers for DNA. We carry DNA, and the possibility for its mutation, into the future. It's as if we're time-travel machines for chromosomes. That seems to be all we're for. (Some mystics have other answers, but Adams doesn't much go there, in any serious way, and neither will we.) And that itself seems inherently absurd. We're caught up in some agenda, if that's the word, that we can never understand...

The universe is fraught with paradox; contradiction is built into the very structure of being. We are equipped, even before birth, with powerful survival instincts. We're designed to fight for survival, to want to live—but like those resentful androids in *Blade Runner*, we are also designed to age and die. "Live!" says the universe. "Except...don't!"

We're asked to survive in a universe that in many respects is hostile to survival: the world is handily equipped with radiation, destructive micro-organisms, predators and sudden scarcities of resources. We're given egos that make us feel important, the center of reality, and then we learn—as Adams reminds us again and again and yet once more—that the universe is unspeakably vast, and we're minute, excruciatingly infinitesimal relative to its vastness. We have universe-sized egos and speck-sized actual importance. That disconnect is hard to take; all those disconnects are hard to take. We tend to adapt to the disconnect with a kind of madness: our obstinate beliefs held in the face of all the evidence to the contrary.

But we can transcend the contradictions, too, Adams seems to suggest. We can become like that old man in the shack. We learn, like that old man, not to take anything seriously. Oh, he takes care of himself and his cat—but he knows better than to impose his human ideas of "sanity" on the universe. He never fixes in any one conceptual framework—and thus he *seems* insane to people whose idea of sanity *is* fixed conceptual frameworks. Effectively, in the context of the consensus reality most people share, he *is* insane, in a relative way. But paradoxically, it's a healthy madness. It's what I would call *philosophical insanity*.

Sometimes, though, the contradictions in life become too difficult to bear. If so, we can adapt by simply shedding them with a kind of tension relief system—that is, we crazily contort our bodies and make a rather odd, repetitious animal-hooting sort of sound: it's called "laughter."

Douglas Adams' sense of humor is itself a kind of suggestion; humor is guidance. Laughter eases tensions, gives you a moment to look around, say to yourself that, after all, here's a helluva mystery. "Slow down, check it out," says laughter. Laugh hysterically so you don't get hysterical.

But our tendency is to get caught up in things—to "identify" with them, as the Buddhists say—so that we lose all perspective, before we have a chance to apply these methods. How do we *remember* to adapt to the absurdity of life with philosophical insanity? To step back, take a breath, not get too caught up? Adams has two words of advice. He mentioned many times that this advice is the main "selling point" of the Hitchhiker's guidebook. It's just two words, found on the bottom part of the book cover:

Don't panic.

John Shirley is the author of numerous novels and books of stories, including the novels *Cellars*, *Wetbones*, *City Come A-Walkin'*, *Eclipse*, *A Splendid Chaos* and the recent Bram Stoker Award-winning *Black Butterflies* from Leisure. He was one of the original cyberpunk writers with William Gibson, Rudy Rucker and Bruce Sterling. He was co-screenwriter of *The Crow* and has written scripts for television series and cable movies. He was lead singer and songwriter for various bands including the punk band SadoNation, the post-punk band Obsession (Celluloid records) and the post-cyberpunk band The Panther Moderns. Mp3s of his work are to be found through links at the fan-created website www.darkecho.com/JohnShirley. His blog is at www.johnshirley.net. His new novels for Del Rey books are *Demons* and *Crawlers*.

John Shirley

A rare interview with Douglas Adams.

Circa 1983 I happened to be in Britain, and took the opportunity to interview Douglas Adams for *Heavy Metal* magazine. HM had nothing to do with rock music, it was and is a magazine of internationally sourced science fiction and fantasy comic strips. They experimented with a journalistic section for a while and there they published my interview. Most Adams fans weren't likely HM readers, and the interview lapsed into obscurity. I recently rediscovered it—and despite the youthfulness I exhibited in my remarks and interviewing, I will not say callowness, I think it's a very good interview, cutting to the heart of his work in much the spirit of the essays in this book . . . so here it is. JS

I N THE MOST RECENT BOOK of the *Hitchhiker's Guide to the Galaxy* series, modestly titled *Life, the Universe and Everything*, Douglas Adams' profoundly incompetent protagonist Arthur Dent finds he's been flung 200 million years into Earth's primeval past, into a part of the world one day to be known as the Islington borough of London, England. Two hundred million years later, its possible to find Douglas Adams in this very Islington. You go up a narrow alley off Islington Green, an alley which Adams rightly describes as looking like "some thug's sure to set about you there." You find a door to an apartment where there should be only soiled wooden crates and cracked cobblestone. You are admitted, and find yourself in a modern, spacious, multi-leveled apartment, replete with bar, theatrical poster prints, skylight, roof garden, and a six-foot-high yellow toothbrush. The toothbrush leans against a bare white wall, and it looks real, like a giant could use it to brush his teeth. Adams is bearishly big, and "once held a job as a bodyguard." He's actually sort of pale and soft-looking but with a classic Brit's aristocratic nose, featuring arched nostrils, and a mind like a wildly careening gyroscope. When he talks, he interjects qualifiers parenthetically and more qualifiers on top of those, and weaves a complex syntax, then brings it all together and by God, it makes sense. His voice is soft, and despite his restless mind he's courteous, and listens to tedious anecdotes [not included here] told by Yours Truly without a visible flicker of impatience.

Adams was born in Cambridge in 1952. He was educated at Brentwood School, Essex, and St. John's College, where he read English. After graduation he wrote for radio and television, as well as authoring, performing, and sometimes directing stage revues in London. He held various odd jobs between the show business gigs, working as a hospital porter, barn builder, chicken-shed cleaner, radio producer and script editor for *Doctor Who*. He is not married, has no children, and "does not wish to hear from anymore Surrey real estate agents."

His newest work in collaboration with John Lloyd, is called *The Meaning of Liff* (that's Liff with two Fs, not Life) and it's a farcical dictionary describing the origin and "actual" meanings of various silly place-names from around England and the U.S. He's also working on a new Hitchhiker's Guide book, so it looks as if the series may be open-ended and why not? Wodehouse wrote scores of Bertie and Jeeves books, and the queen knighted him for it. Adams took my serious questions seriously, not trying to perform during the interview, and only occasionally glanced at his watch.

—JOHN SHIRLEY

JS: According to my information, you were born in 1943 in Madagascar, the son of a West Indian prince and the wife of a British ambassador—an illegitimate child, you nevertheless rose to be one of Britain's foremost cricket batsmen. You received every honor due the best of that profession before retiring from the sport in 1967 as a result of religious convictions which forbade the use of a cricket bat outside the institution of marriage. Is that substantially correct?

DA: Nearly. There are a couple of details I'd like to correct... You got the century right. Not everyone gets the century right. You were more accurate than many—well, a curious thing happened recently. I had a whole batch of letters from this woman who claimed to have written the first two books of Hitchhiker sitting in a bar somewhere in Zambia fifteen years ago! Her letters often seemed to be quite rational, and then suddenly they would sink into two or three lines of rampant paranoia and then become rational again.

JS: This is your public. We all wrote the books at some point. I myself wrote the second book.

DA: Did you? I liked that one best. You did a good job.

JS: In your real life, before the *Hitchhiker's Guide to the Galaxy* radio series began, you were a member of a sort of comedy club in Cambridge. Other members were John Cleese and Eric Idle.

DA: Yes. Footlights Club, which has produced in its day an awful lot of people who went into English comedy but also people who went into broadcasting and theatre generally. The names that spring to mind are Peter Cook, Jonathan Miller, John Cleese, Graham Chapman, Eric Idle. Oxford had their own group which produced Michael Palm, Terry Jones, Allen Rennet, Dudley Moore. I worked for a short time with Graham Chapman, one of the Pythons, but not actually on Python itself on a number of things, most of which failed to see the light of day.

JS: Did you write anything in the way of fiction before *Hitchhiker's*?

DA: Not fiction, no. Sketches. Doing bits and pieces for the odd sketch show on radio. Having a pretty unspectacular career really. I suppose the eighteen months before *Hitchhiker* were the least spectacular. I was having real money problems, couldn't pay the rent, getting really down and very depressed. I actually went and stayed in my parents' home down in Dorset for a while, while I worked out what I was going to do next, and ended up starting the Hitchhiker radio play while I was down there. [Note: the radio plays were written first, and the first two books were adapted from them. Then Adams wrote the third in the series from scratch.]

JS: Are you working on more fiction?

DA: I'm going to write one more Hitchhiker book. My title for the moment—I'm having arguments with my agent, he doesn't like it—is *So Long and Thanks for All the Fish*.

JS: Some of the series reminds me of S.J. Perelman's travel sketches, the acerbity that he would use in describing exotic places.

DA: (dubiously) Hmm...Well I love good comedy writing, because knowing how difficult it is to do, I very much respect those who do it particularly well. And people sometimes say to me, "Do you ever aspire to write a serious book?" And my practiced glib answer to that is, "No, my aspirations are much greater than that, I aspire to write like PG. Wodehouse."

JS: Arthur Dent seems to me a lot like Bertie Wooster, the archetypal Wodehouse creation. He's used like Bertie Wooster, and his un-shakeable but sympathetic denseness resembles Bertie. I assume Wodehouse is an influence.

DA: Yes, he's definitely an influence. But in fact, one of the guides I use when I'm trying to convey the character of Arthur is Simon Jones. Which is not to say that Simon Jones is like Arthur Dent. But he has made the character in his performance so clear to me, I tend to sort of put Simon in his dressing gown there in my head and write what comes from that.

JS: The section of *Restaurant at the End of the Universe* regarding the legions of useless people—"hairdressers, management consultants, telephone sanitizers, and so forth"—castaway on a hostile world and insisting on a Management Efficiency Committee to deal with the problem of building a fire, is reminiscent of Alice's arguments with the functionaries of Wonderland. Is it a deliberate reference to Lewis Carroll?

DA: No, it isn't actually. Lewis Carroll, curiously enough, I read when I was a little kid, and it frightened me to bits and I couldn't bear it since then. A number of people keep on saying that Lewis Carroll uses number forty-two quite a lot [Note: for the mystical significance of forty-two in the Hitchhiker series, read the Hitchhiker series] and find some significance in that. But if I'd used the number thirty-nine other people would have found references in other people's books for that number, and so on and so forth. As far as children's books are concerned, a much stronger influence would be Winnie the Pooh. Because Milne's writing is wonderful—it's easy to read and it's beautifully written, worth having a look at again.

JS: You're now being hyped in the States, as I'm sure you know. How do you feel about that?

DA: Well, what I'd like to be sure doesn't happen—and so far I've managed to resist it—is when the media presentation outstrips the public reaction. That is really what hype is—when there's a sort of credibility gap between what the publicists say and how the public's really responded. But luckily the original public response really came up out of nowhere, and therefore I felt the hype simply kept pace with that. What would be terrible would be if the thing had been launched in the first place in a sort of huge great glare of publicity. But it's grown in response to public demand. I'd be nervous if there'd been a lot of publicity on the first book and everyone had said, "Well it really wasn't worth it, was it?"

JS: How would you feel if some group of air-heads started a religious cult based on your series? After all, it has a number of mystical/comical joke overtones.

DA: I once sat in a cafe in San Francisco and heard a new religion started at the next table just round some poetry this guy had written. On the one hand, yes, I think it would be absurd and ridiculous; on the other hand, I'm no longer surprised at the absurd and ridiculous things people do. I was sitting watching Channel 22 in Los Angeles, an evangelist's program, and it was absolutely frightening—a sort of cross between Dolly Parton and Eichmann. And it's supposed to be religion, but God is hardly ever mentioned—it's all Money and Success and Send Money To This Address and Help us Pay For These Hairdos.

JS: There seems to be, in your series, a kind of tension between an overwhelming sense of a chaotic universe and a yearning for orderly explanations in life. I mean, you make fun of looking for meaning in life but at the same time you're looking for meaning in life.

DA: Well, yes. Just in order to get by from one day to another in life one has to make certain assumptions about the way the world

works. About the way patterns recur. On the other hand, there is
an immense amount we don't know anything about at all. And the
things we take for granted do occasionally break down, and life is
terribly cruel and unfair in the most arbitrary way. And you suddenly realize we don't really understand anything about the way we
operate or why we're here. In order to really understand anything,
you'd need to know everything—which we can't possibly do.

JS: That's relevant to a bit in *Restaurant* where there's a man in a shack
on a deserted planet who allegedly controls the universe—it's never resolved whether he truly does—and he's constantly question-
ing reality on the basis of the universal subjectivity of everyone's
impressions.

DA: That's right, he refuses to accept anything at all as real except
those things he whimsically decides to accept.

JS: Does this represent your own viewpoint?

DA: It doesn't represent my view in terms of what one lives by, but it
represents something I'm aware of and think about.

JS: I have the impression the man in the shack feels everyone is always very isolated and anytime we can communicate anything that
was like what we really meant, it's almost miraculous.

DA: Yes, that's line. We talk about one universe but the universe I live
in is the universe as it is revealed to my own senses—which is absolutely subjective—and the universe you live in is absolutely subjective to you. I imagine you in my mind at the moment and you
imagine me in yours. But in fact we're talking about two universes.

JS: If you keep on like that you'll give me an acid flashback...People
and things get killed wildly in all three of the books. There's car-
nage, and at one point there's a reference to a planet which is used
as a billiard ball in a cosmic game of pool, causing billions of inhabitants to die as it's sunk in the pocket of a black hole. You're fascinated by death, and you're either salaciously fascinated or you're
protesting and very upset about it.

DA: I'm certainly not salacious about it, quite the reverse. No, it's not
a protest, you can't protest against death.

JS: Yeah, who do you make the protest to?

DA: Yes, "I demand not to die!" Wanton, casual, meaningless death—
yes, I do it, like the death of the whale in the first book. I found
that sort of moving, actually, the death of the whale, who's just
arbitrarily called into existence and has about ninety seconds to
work out who he is, what he's doing there, and what his life is all

about, before it ends. I don't know why I keep on doing that, the violence. It's partly, I suppose, to engage sympathy for the people concerned. To engage other people's sympathy or to engage mine, I don't know. What I find upsetting is not the violence as you see it in a film like *Straw Dogs*—which I thought was a very good film— but the violence that you get in the average American cop show where bystanders or people you'd see in the story for a half-minute get shot and no more mention is made of them. I think the death of that whale came to me while I was watching an episode of an American TV show called *Cannon* a few years ago. Some guy who was probably one of the henchmen of the baddies got shot and his only function in the story was to get shot. I began to think, "Well, who is he, where did he come from?" He must have grown up and had a mother and father who sent him off to school and were very proud of him, and suddenly he gets shot on the street and no one's even noticed. That sort of mindless, meaningless violence which nobody even notices is what really upsets me.

JS: So in the books you're reacting against the meaninglessness of random violence—

DA: Yes, but I don't want to make that sound like a statement. I do get very upset by violence or suffering that people I know go through. I get almost unnaturally upset about it.

JS: There was the episode in one of your books where somebody threw a pebble into the brush which started a chain of events that led to the death of the girlfriend of the guy who innocently threw the pebble.

DA: That goes back to the idea of chaos and order, because everything that happened there happened in a perfectly orderly way, following its own little logical progression, but it introduced a completely random event of unpleasant proportions back into the story. It's one of those things one frequently gets confronted by in life, which is the bad experience, the terrible experience, from which it is impossible to learn anything at all. Given the destruction caused by the randomness in the universe, why do we also have to deal with the phone company? It seems unfair we should do it to ourselves, inflicting suffering via the phone company, when we've already got the natural world doing it to us.

JS: What about the charge that most of the effect in British humor derives from the too-easy device of inserting absurd anomalies—the exotic in the banal background like a Martian stepping out of a refrigerator, which you'd see on Monty Python, or the banal in the exotic, like Italian Bistros in Space as in your most recent book. Isn't that too prevalent in English humor?

DA: No, I think it's too prevalent in life. I think we English notice more that goes on. An example of the banal set in the exotic: Go to Sheridan, Wyoming. We just drove from Los Angeles to New York and the countryside in America is fantastically beautiful—the most beautiful part we happened to see was Wyoming. Then to arrive at Sheridan and find such an extraordinarily grotty place—it was inconceivable that people could build a town like that in that setting. Don't they ever look out of their windows? I find that the major difference between the English and the Americans is the Americans lack a sense of irony. Especially after living six months in Los Angeles. It's not the same in New York, of course. Well we went to a restaurant that night in Sheridan, and it was very, very difficult to find anywhere one would actually want to go into. We eventually found this place which didn't have any windows, and it had a really dreadful old stained red carpet, which smelled of old carbolic, and horrible plastic chandeliers dripping all over the place, and some guy playing the electric organ very very slowly and women wearing high heels and ankle socks. We said to one waiter we spoke to, "That scenery out there! The land in which you live is incredible!" And he said, "Oh yeah it's quite nice up there—but have you been to Las Vegas?!" Great.

JS: Americans are obsessed with the artifacts of exploitation and to them that's beauty. Places like Sheridan are the very soul of the country. Were you in L.A. working on the Hitchhiker film?

DA: I was working on a screenplay while I was in Los Angeles. It's very difficult to say anything too clearly at this moment, simply because until you're actually in production you can't know what's happening. Or even when you're in production—only when you've finally got the film can you know what it is you're talking about. At this stage I haven't got a version I'm happy with. What we've got at the moment is me trying to meet them and them trying to meet me and they're not being quite happy and then me not being quite happy with it.

JS: American producers?

DA: Yeah.

JS: A venomous breed. Mark my words, five years from now you'll be writing bitter satire about Hollywood producers.

DA: I have started work on the Hitchhiker computer adventure game.

JS: What about an animated version of Hitchhiker?

DA: I've never been keen on that idea, because my impulse has always been with these fantastical situations to try—I don't say I'm always successful—but to try and make them as real and solid and concrete as possible. And I think you're really stacking the odds against yourself if you go into animation. Because it tends to emphasize the fantastical nature of the events. I want the events to be fantastical but to appear to be as real as possible.

JS: What about the hieroglyphic versions? Cuneiform? Stained-glass? Comic books?

DA: Comic books? What would I do with comic books? Either I'm going to devote my time to writing stories for comic books, which I don't want to do, or go hand it over to somebody else. I don't want to do that.

JS: So you like to maintain control over Hitchhiker projects?

DA: Oh yeah. But on the screenplay I have what is known as "consultation rights," which is not the same as artistic control. Frankly you have to be Warren Beatty or someone to get artistic control.

JS: Do you read science fiction?

DA: Not very much. I've got piles of science fiction books next door largely because [sighing] people keep on giving them to me. The best ones I've enjoyed tremendously, like *A Canticle For Liebowitz.* And one of the people I came across is Robert Sheckley, who is tremendous. When I read a collection of Robert Sheckley stories for the first time I really felt my nose well-and-true put out of joint because I thought, "This is precisely what I wanted to try to do and he's done it a great deal better."

JS: How do you feel about drugs?

DA: I'm a clean-living boy. I used to occasionally smoke a little dope. Half a dozen times a year. I meet people who say, "Hey, what are you on when you write that stuff?" You can't write well unless you're under control. Particularly writing fantasy.

JS: The scourge of the universe in *Life, the Universe and Everything* were the people of Krikket, who were so incredibly xenophobic and ultraprovincial they wanted to obliterate the whole universe so they could have their isolated idyll undisturbed…

DA: The idea behind that was to create a race of villains whose behavior was utterly villainous by the standards of anybody else, but according to their own precepts they are behaving well, behaving decently, behaving morally.

JS: So villains are never completely villainous if you see things from their viewpoint. Is that the message here?

DA: Oh, I don't think there's a message.

JS: I insist on finding a message in it!

DA: Very well. That's a message, then.

JS: Anyway, your books are therapeutic. When you make great humor out of the senseless patterns of random violence in life, you make life more acceptable and tolerable, because you make it possible to laugh it off.

DA: Yes, I recognize that as being at work in my books.

JS: Thanks for that therapy. And the ordeal is now over, Thanks, Mr. Adams.

Special Thanks to David Haddock for finding a copy of this "lost interview"!

Adam-Troy Castro

Another Fine Mess

Dent: Well then who's on first?
Prefect: Yes.
Dent: I mean the fellow's name.
Prefect: Who.
Dent: The guy on first.
Prefect: Who.
Dent: The first baseman.
Prefect: Who.
Dent: The guy playing...
Prefect: Who is on first!
Dent: I'm asking YOU who's on first.

THE HITCHHIKER'S GUIDE TO THE GALAXY comes down to a cross between two phenomena I call the Laurel and Hardy Paradox and the Two-Guys-In-A-Spaceship-Getting-In-Trouble-Again-Story.

They're really two separate aspects of the same phenomenon, since the Laurel and Hardy Paradox is in and of itself a key element of the average Two-Guys-In-A-Spaceship-Getting-In-Trouble-Again story. But the Paradox is such an integral element that it deserves its own separate explanation.

To wit:

You have these dudes, Laurel and Hardy. (Or Abbott and Costello, or the Three Stooges, but let's not drive ourselves crazy here. It's called the Laurel and Hardy Paradox, not the Laurel and Hardy Paradox with Footnotes. Accept it.) Anyway, Laurel and Hardy are screw-ups of the highest order, who regularly demolish their own lives with hilarious self-inflicted disasters. In most of the one- or two-reel shorts that represent their best work, they take a relatively minor problem, like fixing a boat, or delivering a piano, or installing a rooftop aerial, and through hard work and the diligent application of escalating incompetence succeed in reducing every breakable surface around them to absolute rubble.

The Paradox is not that this happens to them. We can see why it happens to them. It has to happen to them.

The Paradox is that it doesn't happen to them sooner.

You see, though the pair are most frequently seen as vagrants, many Laurel and Hardy shorts begin with the two buddies as homeowners or storekeepers or furniture movers or carpenters or police officers or middle-class family men: in short, as respected members of society, with jobs and personal assets and families, which they have somehow managed to accumulate over what must have been years of dedicated struggle. In the thirty minutes of mayhem that follows, Hardy's home will become a smoking ruin, or the car they share will be cut in half with a bandsaw, or the appliance store they run will be stripped to the walls by a thief they're too stupid and/or distracted to stop. The impossibility, given the level of intelligence they display during this thirty minutes of escalating disaster, is just how they managed to maintain the peaceful lives they evidently led up to this point. It just doesn't seem to be in them.

And we know it's more than just happening to catch them on a bad day, because the next hundred times we catch a Laurel and Hardy film we find them playing, for all intents and purposes, the same two guys, who will once again start from an upright position and once again bring the world down upon themselves.

It's a paradox, all right.

It's also a key element of their appeal, and the appeal of a certain hallowed subgenre of our second phenomenon, the Two-Guys-In-A-Spaceship-Getting-In-Trouble-Again-Story.

This subgenre has a long and distinguished past, going back at least seventy years. It's been done comedically and it's been done tragically. In every event, the "Again" part of the equation is vital; the subgenre becomes even more compelling when the two hapless guys in question are folks we see again and again, getting in trouble again and again.

The fascination lies in the fact that it keeps happening: in the fact that the universe just doesn't seem to like them all that much.

Ross Rocklynne wrote one such series in the 1930s. One guy was a wily interplanetary criminal, Edward Deverel; the other was Lieutenant John Cobie, the interplanetary cop determined to bring him down. The inevitable confrontations between this proto-Kimble and proto-Gerard were always complicated by the bizarre alien environments where they met, which always trapped them in awful situations that forced them to team up. The most famous story in this series is "The Men and the Mirror," in which the pair topples over the edge of a gigantic concave mirror many kilometers in diameter; the nearly frictionless surface acts as a sliding pond, obliging the pair to whoosh all the way down one slope and then almost all the way up the other, dozens of times over the course of many hours, losing sufficient momentum on each and every swing to know that they'll eventually be stranded, without hope of rescue or escape, at the very bottom. The solution that saved their lives hinged on recognizing their predicament as a form of pendulum. The physics don't quite work, but that doesn't matter. It's still a neat story, in part because it's only the most recent of several such predicaments the pair has experienced, and they inevitably complain at length about the perverse glee the universe seems to take in saddling them with such problems.

Isaac Asimov produced his own pair of hapless guys in Powell and Donovan, spacefaring troubleshooters for the corporation U.S. Robots and Mechanical Men, who couldn't go anywhere without the inherent ambiguities in the laws governing artificial intelligence forcing a major crisis. In one such tale, "Runaround," they're stuck on Mercury waiting for their robot to deliver an important element before life support fails, and find themselves obliged to figure out why the robot is gallivanting around pools of molten metal, singing in drunken verse. They solve the mystery, of course. But not without complaining at length about their luck, and not without going on to an immediate sequel where they find themselves in trouble once again.

Robert Sheckley contributed several tales involving Richard Gregor and Frank Arnold of the AAA Planetary Decontamination Service, who like Deverel and Cobie, and Powell and Donovan, couldn't go anywhere without becoming entrapped in some absurd life-or-death situation. In one such tale, they equip their vessel with a device that will manufacture anything they need on their journey—but only, they discover far too late, one of each. Slowly starving, because the device includes food in its list of items it will no longer produce, Gregor and Arnold come up with an elegant solution…though, again, not without making matters even worse.

I produced my own pair of starfaring shlimazels in the form of inter-galactic criminals Ernst Vossoff and Karl Nimmitz, who just couldn't seem to travel a light year in any direction without encountering something along the lines of a carnivorous pink bunny the size of a planet.

Not all of these spacefaring characters were as stupid as Laurel and Hardy. Some qualified as geniuses. But their bad luck compensated. They just couldn't go anywhere, or do anything, without the very structure of the universe rearranging itself into a gigantic cannon aimed at their very heads. The cosmos just wanted to screw with them, that's all. The paradox is the same one that marks Laurel and Hardy: that they previously managed to muddle along somehow, living their lives, until disasters began to proliferate, one after another.

Which brings us to Arthur Dent and Ford Prefect.

Let's examine Arthur.

He's an okay guy, isn't he? A bit prissy, a bit short on adaptability, a bit below average when it comes to any ability to enjoy strange new places and great awe-inspiring wonders, a bit unlucky when it comes to the opposite sex, but an okay guy, all in all: a guy who, before the fateful moment when we entered his orbit, seemed to have done pretty okay by himself. He was living a comfortable middle-class existence in a comfortable middle-class home, which means he also had a comfortable middle-class income, a résumé and a history of paying the bills on time. It may have been a dull life—given Arthur's personality, it pretty much would have had to be—but up until the moment we first see him it was also a life that never never involved lying down in the mud to stop a bulldozer, or being whisked into outer space without having the chance to change out of his bathrobe.

By all the evidence available to Arthur at that moment, Ford Prefect was pretty much the same kind of fellow. Oh, he had some quirks all right (that name, for instance), but he was also the kind of fellow who, stranded on a primitive planet with thousands of subcultures and billions of sentients to choose from, would pick Arthur Dent as best friend. Their relationship was quite comfortable by the earthbound Arthur's standards: "Most of it seemed to make sense at the time." Which is to say, it never involved the kind of weirdness that would have made Arthur flail his arms in panic while screeching like a little girl. There had been no alien death fleets, no paranoid androids, no two-headed hipsters, no falling whales: no crises, really. Their lives up to that point had comprised, shall we say, a mind-boggling dearth of incident.

(I'm sure Arthur would say differently. They had been friends long enough that there must have been some incident, somewhere in the shared past, where they went to a cricket game and had all sorts of amusing misadventures trying to find the car afterward. Arthur no doubt whined through the whole thing that this was the sort of wildly improbable thing that only happened to him. He probably considered it a great anecdote. It was, prior to the destruction of the Earth by the poetry-spouting Vogons, about as exciting as his life ever got.)

From the moment the series begins, when they become two-guys-in-a-series-of-spaceships-getting-into-trouble-again, they will not be ejected out one airlock without immediately tumbling into another one. They won't be able to escape one set of demented aliens without immediately encountering another. They won't be able to process one lunatic improbability before being asked to swallow a second.

How did guys with this kind of luck ever manage to live a relatively sane existence for so long?

We know the answer in Ford Prefect's case. He was a researcher for the *Hitchhiker's Guide*; his life, before being stranded on Earth, was awash with lunacy of the same scale that awaited Arthur. His terrestrial existence was, at best, a brief respite between cosmic disasters—or, given what passes for terrestrial existence, a prime example of them.

Explaining Arthur's prior immunity is a little more difficult, but Douglas Adams does provide us with a clue: one that explains not only the central facet of his existence but also the mysteries of the Laurel and Hardy paradox as well.

Early in their post-Earth adventures, Ford and Arthur encounter the crew of the starship *Heart of Gold*. Improbably enough, that crew includes Tricia McMillan, whom Arthur once met and tried to proposition...and Zaphod Beeblebrox, who came between them. The incident doesn't seem to have had all that much substance to it, but it was nevertheless vivid enough to stick in Arthur's incident-starved memory, and the bland summary Arthur walked away with (he lost a pretty girl to a more rakish guy), utterly missed the point of what happened. Which was—

—even when his life was dull, Arthur was already having close encounters with creatures from other planets.

Not just Zaphod. Ford, too.

Okay, granted, you might be able to attribute Arthur's cocktail party encounter with Zaphod to the effects of the Infinite Improbability Drive, which may have already been in Zaphod's hands at the time, but that's stretching things a mite—and even if true, would have been just one contributing factor to the unlikelihood, not its ultimate explanation. Not when you consider that Arthur's longstanding friendship with Ford began years and years earlier, long before Zaphod even got his hands on the dang thing.

The fact is, with or without that aggravating factor, Arthur still experienced something totally mind-blowing, more than once.

But he walked away with an understanding that was just plain banal.

He failed to notice, that's all.

There can't be any *Guide* devotee who finds this surprising in light of the man's post-Earth behavior, but few have extrapolated the epiphany to the rest of his terrestrial life. In other words, maybe his existence wasn't so dull after all. Maybe his existence, before the arrival of the Vogons, was just as filled with terror and absurdity as his existence afterward. Maybe his postman came from Saturn. Maybe the desk-bound secretary he said hello to every morning was an octopus from the waist down. Maybe there was a space warp in his closet. Maybe he wandered, dull-eyed and oblivious, past a thousand little armageddons with every step he took, and never paid attention until he encountered the first that affected him directly.

Maybe, like that experienced by Laurel and Hardy and the various Two Guys In A Succession of Spaceships, the deceptive order Arthur thought he saw, before fate changed everything, was just an illusion. Maybe that illusion covered any number of cosmic miracles and earth-shattering disasters and insanely improbable plot twists, and was only effective because of his blindered perspective.

In short, maybe he was just like the rest of us.

Adam-Troy Castro has written four novels and over seventy short stories, including the Stoker nominee "Baby Girl Diamond," the Hugo and Nebula nominee "The Funeral March of the Marionettes" and the Nebula nominee "Of A Sweet Slow Dance in the Wake of Temporary Dogs." His most recent paperback, *Vossoff and Nimmitz*, sneakily plugged in the body of his contribution to this anthology, is an exercise in science fictional silliness that just happens to be dedicated to Douglas Adams. When not hitchhiking to strange destinations, Adam-Troy lives in Miami with his long-suffering wife Judi and a collection of insane cats that includes Uma Furman and Meow Farrow.

Amy Berner

Words to Live By

A man named Robert Fulghum once wrote a book called
All I Really Need to Know I Learned in Kindergarten. It
sold approximately a billion trillion copies, and launched
a million sayings and a hundred other books all starting
with "All I ever really need to know I learned . . . ." Now, I
never read his book, and it may be brilliant. But I doubt
it. Kindergarten is far too limiting a place to learn everything you need to know—not if you want to function as
an adult. He should have called it *I Haven't Learned a
Damn Thing Since First Grade*, which says essentially the
same thing and makes the utter ridiculousness of it a bit
more obvious. I'm ranting, I know, but there is a point.
Life is complicated. There are very few genuine sources
of everything you really need to know. It just so happens
that Hitchhiker's is one of them.

"You know," said Arthur, "it's at times like this, when I'm trapped in a Vogon airlock with a man from Betelgeuse, and about to die of asphyxiation in deep space, that I really wish I'd listened to what my mother told me when I was young."

"Why, what did she tell you?"

"I don't know, I didn't listen."

—*The Hitchhiker's Guide to the Galaxy*

I WAS FOURTEEN when my mother gave me my first copies of *The Hitchhiker's Guide to the Galaxy* and *The Restaurant at the End of the Universe*. The third and fourth volumes of the inappropriately named trilogy soon followed. She had already read and loved the books, and she knew that they were right up my science fiction bookwormish alley. When I was younger, she had repeatedly tried to get my nose out of whatever book I was reading, suggesting that I play outside when the weather in Wisconsin was actually worth playing in. By the time that I'd become a teenager, she'd given up on this tactic (it never worked, and I was turning out okay anyway—besides, we lived in Southern California by this point, and nice days were plentiful).

Mom was pretty darn smart. Heck, she was the one who started me out in the realm of science fiction in the first place, fostering my interest in television shows such as *Star Trek* and *Doctor Who* and planning mother-daughter weekends at science fiction conventions. Not only did she enjoy these television shows and books herself, but I believe that she'd much rather I focus on a genre that forced me to think and question rather than be spoon-fed mindless entertainment (which is probably why I never got that Atari system).

My initial memories of the Hitchhiker's Guide series are intertwined with memories of my mother: how I would burst out laughing my first time through, and she'd poke her head into my room wondering which part I had just read; how the number forty-two became a part of our daily lives; how we never looked at dolphins quite the same way again when we saw them at Sea World or the Mirage in Las Vegas. When a friend lent us VHS tapes of the BBC television show, it was cause for celebration and copious amounts of popcorn (with extra butter—I was, after all, raised in Wisconsin).

I've reread the Hitchhiker's series countless times over the years, and I have never stopped finding joy and laughter in them. I still love the silly irreverence, and the satire remains as fresh and true today as it did then (even if I no longer actually wear a digital watch). But there is more to these books than just comedy. Douglas Adams snuck in some amazingly good advice. It didn't register to my fourteen-year-old mind, but as I've revisited the series, I have found that there is more wisdom to be found among the jokes than I gave it credit for. Sneaky, wasn't he?

Mom was too. In between giggling madly over the descriptions of the Disaster Area concert or Vogon poetry, my mother had to have hoped that her daughter might learn a little something. It's a case in which the saying that's been attributed to everything from baseball to cooking can be applied quite well: "Everything I ever needed to know, I learned from The Hitchhiker's Guide to the Galaxy."

Well, okay, maybe not *everything*. The books didn't teach me how to tie my shoes or clean my room (the latter of which I never quite mastered—Mom eventually gave up on that one). But in taking some things from these books to heart, I've found I can make my life a little better.

"TIME IS AN ILLUSION. LUNCHTIME DOUBLY SO."

Time, as you may have heard, is relative. In this case, there aren't any complicated scientific formulas involved. It's all about how you look at it.

Even when Arthur Dent's mind is distracted by the thought of his home being demolished by a bulldozer to make way for a new bypass, he is a little startled at the idea of vast quantities of beer at lunchtime. It seems disturbingly improper to him. Like most Earthlings, Arthur believes (at the time) that everything should fit in comfortable little categories and follow familiar patterns, and none of those categories or patterns accounted for Ford's order of six pints of bitter for just the two of them. We are, after all, creatures of habit. We follow customs and traditions and etiquette. Dessert always follows the meal. Only wear white shoes between Memorial Day and Labor Day (although I've never understood that summertime-only white shoe rule).

Anyway, what is this "lunchtime" that Ford deems illusory? For some, it's a break in the day that we take to nab some food before we dive back into the whirlwind of our everyday lives—a catch-your-breath kind of break that some people skip altogether. (I'm guilty of this on a regular basis, something I know my mother would *not* approve of.) For others, it is a midday oasis, a time for a leisurely meal. Back in grade school, lunch was my time for burying my nose in a book while chewing on my peanut butter and honey sandwich. Lunchtime can have many uses. Everything is what you make of it.

What we believe an occasion is "supposed" to be, or how we choose to categorize it, is all in our minds. Who says that you can't have scrambled eggs or pancakes for supper? Mom and I did that all the time; we called it "brupper" (a combination of "breakfast" and "supper").

The satisfaction that comes with breaking one of these categorization rules is extraordinary, whether it's done on a whim or for good reason. Give it a try. You might discover that it really is okay to eat dessert first, try brupper and, when the circumstances warrant it (for example, to fulfill the need for a muscle relaxant before going through a matter transference beam), drink three pints of beer with lunch.

"I'D FAR RATHER BE HAPPY THAN RIGHT ANY DAY"

"In this replacement Earth we're building they've given me Africa to do and of course I'm doing it all with fjords again because I happen to like them and I'm old-fashioned enough to feel that they give a lovely baroque feel to the continent. And they tell me it's not equatorial enough. Equatorial!" He gave a hollow laugh. "What does it matter? Science has achieved some wonderful things, of course, but I'd far rather be happy than right any day."
—SLARTIBARTFAST, *The Hitchhiker's Guide to the Galaxy*

Slartibartfast was happy with his fjords, and he liked to use them in his designs. Oh, but that's not How It Is Done. Set parameters and guides must be followed.

Boring! Fjords are nifty. Sure, they aren't traditionally found on an equatorial continent, but a little pizzazz can be nice. What could it hurt? Who says that Africa needs to look all proper and equatorial?

I can guarantee that if my mother had been present, she'd have told Slartibartfast to go ahead and add as many fjords as he felt like and to heck with its equatorialness. She was neither prim nor proper. She'd much rather add a little fun to a situation. For example, she taught me by example that jumping up and down and yelling at baseball games and other sporting events was not only acceptable but highly encouraged. She's the only person I've ever met who looked good wearing a "cheesehead" hat. She drove old Volkswagen beetles because she liked them, and decorated them as she saw fit (her last Beetle had a San Diego Chargers logo and lightning bolts in the back window).

To her, standing out from the crowd was a good thing, whether it was the proper thing to do or not. This isn't to say that she was an impractical woman or embarrassingly outlandish, despite my common protestations of "Oh, Mom" as her somewhat more conservative offspring (of the two of us, I was by far the quieter one). She was a very practical and logical person. But when the situation was something for which a moderate approach wasn't important in the grand scheme of, well, anything, she'd squeeze all the fun out of it that she could. She'd clap or sing along to music and she'd go all out when putting together a costume. And, at gift-giving times, there was always a "frivle" (our word for a frivolous gift) included with the more practical items.

There is a time to do what other people deem to be "right" or proper, and there are times when you just don't have to. You can get up and dance at a concert. You can yell at the top of your lungs when the home team hits a home run. You can add ruffles and sequins to a dress, and you can add fjords to a continent.

I'm getting better at letting go of unimportant conventions, but this was something Mom was much better at than I am. I've mastered the sports fan behavior model, but that one was easy. There are some things that I never quite caught up to her on. She'd wear the bright pink sweater while I wore the black. She'd wear a sparkling pin on her shirt just because she liked it, and she preferred garnets to the traditional diamonds. She'd jump on the dance floor long before I did.

She always tried to help me push the envelope, to do something a little different. Making roses out of satin instead of buying a bunch of boring fake flowers. Adding a touch of pink sequins to my blue and black solo dance costume. Giving me lip gloss that made my lips extra-shiny. Just because.

Bit by bit, I try to let myself add a few fjords. I give myself permission to be goofy. I buy a bright scarf because it's a pretty color. I wear outfits to work that lean closer to whimsical than conservative and business-like. I buy random objects for my house because I think that they are nifty; instead of a traditional dining room table, I bought a bright orange bar, an antique from the early sixties. Mom would have fully approved of this, and likely would have come over for many a glass of wine.

Mom would've covered every coastline with fjords and cliffs if given the chance. Because they're fun, and what's the point of doing anything if you aren't going to enjoy it? I think I might go a little fjord-happy myself.

"KNOW WHERE YOUR TOWEL IS"

The Hitchhiker's Guide to the Galaxy has a few things to say on the subject of towels.

A towel, it says, is about the most massively useful thing an interstellar hitchhiker can have.... Hence a phrase that has passed into hitchhiking slang, as in "Hey, you sass that hoopy Ford Prefect? There's a frood who really knows where his towel is."

—Information from the Guide in *The Hitchhiker's Guide*
to the Galaxy

It helps to have something to get you through the day, something you can cling to, especially when surrounded by nothing resembling normality. We all need a little extra support to get through life in this wacky universe.

For those hitchhiking across the galaxy, nothing does the job of getting the traveler through the day better than a trusty towel—according to the *Guide*, a towel "is about the most massively useful thing an interstellar hitchhiker can have." There is quite a long list of uses for towels (including wrapping yourself in it, lying on it or under it, using it as a flag or weapon and the shocking idea of using one to dry off), but at heart, the towel serves as a security blanket. It's something that gives you confidence and/or comfort. It fosters an attitude that, no matter what life, the universe and everything throws at you, you can withstand it.

My original "towel" was a vaguely panda-looking teddy bear with overly large orange eyes named Theodore. Not the most original of towel-esque items, true, but that bear was important to me. For more years than I care to admit, as long as I knew where Theodore was, or that Theodore was nearby, then everything was okay. Mom treated Theodore with all the respect due to such a central facet of my life, to the point that she'd turn around when we were halfway out of the city if he'd been mistakenly left behind. More than once. Even when I became too old for such supposed foolishness, we both referred to him as if he was a member of the family. (For the record, Theodore currently resides in my living room where he lords over the sofa, and he still has every stitch Mom sewed into him during the many necessary repairs.)

Your towel—whatever your towel may be—is something important. Honestly, that little plush bear is still my towel in a lot of ways, as I don't think I could ever part with him. I'm okay with this. Because, as galactic hitchhikers read in the *Guide*, a fellow who can "struggle against terrible odds,,win through, and still knows where his towel is, is clearly a man to be reckoned with." I've got Theodore. Everything will be fine. And I'm a gal to be reckoned with.

THE KNACK TO FLYING IS LEARNING HOW TO THROW YOURSELF AT THE GROUND AND MISS.

There is an art, it says, or rather, a knack to flying. The knack lies in learning how to throw yourself at the ground and miss.... All it requires is simply the ability to throw yourself forward with all your weight, and willingness not to mind that it's going to hurt. That is, it's going to hurt if you fail to miss the ground.
—Information from the Guide in *Life, the Universe and Everything*

Everybody wants to fly. Zooming about, unfettered by pesky things like gravity, is a common dream. And hey, it's a good one.

I've always seen this idea as having to do with achieving your dreams. Making a huge leap forward means risking doing a huge belly flop into the ground, and most people do fail to miss the ground when they try. The ground is large and hard and unforgiving, and it hurts when you fail to miss it. The point is that you have to try. You have to be willing to risk that belly flop if you want to soar.

Mom was always proudest of me when I took a risk, and she was always there to support me when I did. If I failed, she would be there to pick me up. But when I put myself out there and jumped and missed the ground, I think she was even more thrilled than I was. I leaped offa very tall cliff when, as a fifteen-year-old who didn't think of herself as all that great of a dancer, I decided to audition for a Superbowl halftime show. When my number was announced as one of those who had made it into the show, I could hear my mother's scream of delight from the far-away sidelines.

Anybody can fly. Supposedly, the trick is to "have your attention momentarily distracted at the crucial moment." This isn't anywhere close to easy. A lot of the time, the mantra in our brains sounds something like "I have to do this right" or "I have to succeed." Listening to it, it's hard to think of anything but how important it is to do so. For me, I've had far better luck when I just do. By overthinking, it's all too easy to flounder.

The Guide also advises not to think too hard about the thing you want to do. Just allow it to happen as if it were going to anyway. Over-trying can be the death of whatever it is that you are attempting. After all, it was Zaphod's be-cool viewpoint on life that led him to being Galactic president (although his invention of the Pan Galactic Gargle Blaster probably helped).

Most importantly, as the Guide tells us, it is vitally important to not believe anyone who says, "Good God, you can't possibly be flying!" If you do, they will suddenly be right. Believe in yourself, and don't let anyone convince you otherwise.

"DON'T PANIC"

I like the cover. "Don't Panic." It's the first helpful or intelligible thing anyone's said all day.
—Arthur Dent, *The Hitchhiker's Guide to the Galaxy*

There are times that I wish everyone had a book with the words "DON'T PANIC" written on the cover in large, friendly letters. We forget something Ford knows as fact: the galaxy's a fun place.

Sure, there can be perfectly reasonable reasons for a good panic, such as losing your cat, being stranded on a desert island or being picked up by an alien spacecraft after your planet has been destroyed to make way for a hyperspace bypass. But even in those cases, what good does panicking accomplish? Lashing out, yelling and running around in circles does nothing to help a situation. It's more likely to make people look at you funny.

It can be hard for a measly human like me to follow Ford's and Zaphod's example and "Be cool," not to mention "Relax." I can't help getting stressed, and relaxing still isn't something I do easily. Emotions take hold and banish reason to an airlock for a while. I have to consciously tell myself, "Don't panic." And it works because I know that I don't need to panic.

There's a reserve in me that Mom fostered, a confidence that I can get through anything because she always believed that I could. No matter what challenges we faced, she never doubted that we could surpass them. She taught me that, no matter what, there is always a way out. Even if the probability is two to the power of two hundred and seventy-six thousand, seven hundred and nine to one against.

When the odds are that high, or when things look extra grim, panicking is a natural reaction. But as much as a brain might scream otherwise, it's a heck of a lot more productive to look at a situation without the flailing. And oddly enough, the probability is fairly decent (far better than that of being picked up within thirty seconds of being shot out into space) that there is a solution for what ails you.

I've been working as an event planner for years now, which is the most panic-ridden industry known to humanity (really, the amount of panic elicited by party planning in some people could power Magrathea, as any event or wedding planner will attest). These two simple words have kept me sane, because 99.99% of the time, there is a way through any crisis. This advice alone is worth a planet's weight in gold. Just like Mom's advice always was.

Every time I dive back into the Hitchhiker's Guide to the Galaxy series, I feel a little bit as if my mother is still at my shoulder. I'll always be grateful to her for introducing these books to me. They've become a part of my "towel" in life, like "brupper" and "frivles," and as long as I have them handy, I have a part of my mother with me.

Thanks, Mom.

Amy Berner has a not-so-slight obsession with the science fiction and fantasy genres. Using what spare time her "day job" and her cats let her have, Amy pops up all over the place with reviews, essays and short stories. Amy is also a contributing author to the *Five Seasons of Angel* anthology. She is a regular columnist for Dark Worlds (www. darkworlds.com) and lives in San Diego, California.

Maria Alexander

"Goodnight, Marvin"

Goodbye, and thanks for all the fish. . . .

May 12, 2001

This is a very sad day.

I woke up this morning and got ready to see the press screening of *Shrek* with my friend Abbie. I was completely unaware that something singular had happened in the world—in *my* world—the day before and a strange nostalgia fogged my head. For the first time in nearly sixteen years, I put on a very special shirt: a baseball jersey with cobalt blue sleeves. On the front of the white, see-through part of the jersey, it says, "Don't Panic"; on the back it reads, "Re-elect Zaphod Beeblebrox." My mother made that shirt for my fifteenth birthday. I wore it this morning because I suddenly felt like it for no apparent reason.

I was (and still am) a huge Douglas Adams fan. I loved everything the man said and wrote. He single-handedly shaped my sense of humor, made me an Anglophile, and crowned me Queen of Geekdom at my junior high and high school. At band camp, my friends and I even wore towels slung over our shoulders and asked others, "Do you know where your towel is?" We would squint at the other band geeks, saying, "But there aren't any real people here at all!" We were hopeless nerds. Yet, we were unique.

I couldn't wait to get a picture of Douglas Adams. I had the biggest, most awful crush on him. Once I did get his picture, I was very disappointed. My mother found me frowning over it in the *TV Guide*.

"What's wrong?" she asked.

"He's old and tall and silly looking," I lamented.

My mother shrugged. "Well, honey, sometimes men are like that."

I discovered him in my early teens when I was listening to NPR. That's when I first heard the banjo strains that opened each episode of the *Hitchhiker's Guide to the Galaxy* radio series. Suddenly, life in a joyless religious home was not so bad. He was shockingly blasphemous, with all his tidbits about God; I tried somehow to reconcile my beliefs with how much I enjoyed him, but it never worked. Still, I listened. And I laughed.

I recorded every episode onto tapes that are now brittle and dusty. To this day, I keep them in a wobbly shoe box, even though I bought the official BBC tapes long ago. My little sister once copied over part of Episode Four with Michael Jackson songs. Just after I assured her that there was "a special place in heaven for little sisters," my mother walked in. If it had only been a few minutes later, I would have been an only child again.

But Douglas Adams did so much more than *Hitchhiker's Guide*. He wrote five HG books altogether, two Dirk Gently novels (which inspired my novelette *Samantha Blazes: Psychic Detective of L.A.*), *The Meaning of Liff* and more.

I once sent him a "belated birthday" letter—somewhere around three months after his birthday. I wanted to make it a habit, but I forgot more often than not. I told him in the letter about the "Don't Panic" shirt, and said that I hadn't worn it in years because it was "entirely see-through." (You could see my bra. It embarrassed me to death as a teen.) I wanted to make him laugh because his insane sense of humor taught a thirteen-year-old girl how to laugh when life betrayed her. His humor and irreverence gave her a chance to enjoy life when faith and family failed.

This morning, we saw *Shrek* and I laughed a lot—something I do quite a bit these days. I went home afterward to write. But this evening, Abbie called me to tell me that Douglas Adams died yesterday of a heart attack. He was only forty-nine. When we hung up, I cried. And I cried. I didn't know him, as some of you did. Maybe he was too old and tall and silly, but I loved him anyway in my own special way. He is a part of me and always will be. And I think it was his ghost whispering to me as I dressed this morning, saying, "Well, now that I'm dead, let's have a look at you in that see-through shirt, shall we?"

Goodnight, Marvin. At least now that pain in all the diodes down your left side has stopped. But I will really, really miss you.

Maria Alexander has committed a number of literary crimes—against Gothic.net, *Chiaroscuro* magazine, *Paradox* magazine and other publications. She's been fined with several Honorable Mentions by the *Year's Best Horror & Fantasy*, appearances on the Preliminary Ballot for the Stoker Award and being a Finalist in the 2003 Moondance Short Fiction Competition sponsored by Coppola and Oprah. In 2005, more of her stories will skulk doggedly in anthologies by Penguin and ROC Books. You can find a full rap sheet at www.thehandless-poet.com. She dwells marginally in Los Angeles with two ungrateful cats and a fish who hates you.

If you are interested in the works of Douglas Adams, you may like to join ZZ9 Plural Z Alpha, the official **Hitchhiker's Guide to the Galaxy Appreciation Society**, founded in 1980.

For details of this fan-run club visit www.zz9.org or send a SAE/IRC to:

> ZZ9 Plural Z Alpha
> c/o Wedges Farmhouse
> Bashurst Hill
> Horsham
> West Sussex
> RH13 0PE

Printed in the United States
by Baker & Taylor Publisher Services